Oxford
Correspondence
Workbook

A. Ashley

OXFORD
UNIVERSITY PRESS

OXFORD

UNIVERSITY PRESS

Great Clarendon Street, Oxford OX2 6DP

Oxford University Press is a department of the University of Oxford.
It furthers the University's objective of excellence in research, scholarship,
and education by publishing worldwide in

Oxford New York

Auckland Bangkok Buenos Aires Cape Town Chennai
Dar es Salaam Delhi Hong Kong Istanbul Karachi Kolkata
Kuala Lumpur Madrid Melbourne Mexico City Mumbai Nairobi
São Paulo Shanghai Taipei Tokyo Toronto

Oxford and *Oxford English* are registered trade marks of
Oxford University Press in the UK and in certain other countries

© Oxford University Press 2003

ISBN 0 19 457214 5

Printed in China

Contents

1
Letters, faxes, and emails

1 Letters: true or false?

Read the following statements and decide which are true and which are false.
Mark the true ones 'T' and the false ones 'F' in the spaces provided.

1 ☐ If a letter begins with the *recipient's* name, e.g. *Dear Mr Ross*, it will close with *Yours faithfully*.

2 ☐ The abbreviation *c.c.* stands for *correct carbons*.

3 ☐ If you were writing a letter to Mr Peter Smith, the salutation would be *Dear Mr Peter Smith*.

4 ☐ The head of a company in the UK is known as the *president*.

5 ☐ In *the USA*, it is correct to open a letter with the salutation *Gentlemen*.

6 ☐ In *the UK*, a date written *2.6.05* means *6 February 2005*.

7 ☐ If a secretary signs a letter and the signature is followed by *p.p. Daniel Harris*, it means that the secretary is signing on behalf of Daniel Harris.

8 ☐ The term *plc* after a UK company's name, e.g. *Hathaway plc*, stands for *Public Limited Corporation*.

9 ☐ The term *Ltd* after a UK company's name means *limited liability*.

10 ☐ If you do not know whether a female correspondent is married or not, it is correct to use the courtesy title *Ms* instead of *Miss* or *Mrs*, e.g. *Ms Tessa Groves*.

11 ☐ This address is an example of blocked style.

```
Peter Voss
Oberlweinfeldweg 33
5207 Therwil
Switzerland
```

12 ☐ It is always impolite to close a letter *Best wishes*.

2 Order of addresses

Write out the following names and addresses in the correct order. Use the blocked style.

EXAMPLE Search Studios Ltd / Leeds / LS4 8QM / Mr L. Scott / 150 Royal Avenue

```
Mr L. Scott
Search Studios Ltd
150 Royal Avenue
Leeds
LS4 8QM
```

1 Warwick House / Soundsonic Ltd / London / 57–59 Warwick Street / SE23 1JF

2 Piazza Leonardo da Vinci 254 / Managing Director / I-20133 / Milano / Sig. D. Fregoni / Fregoni S.p.A. /

3 Bente Spedition GmbH / Herr Heinz Bente / D-6000 Frankfurt 1 / Feldbergstr. 30 / Chairman

4 Sportique et Cie / 201 rue Sambin / The Sales Manager / F–21000 Dijon
5 Intercom / E-41006 Sevilla / 351 Avda Luis de Morales / Chief Accountant /
   Mrs S. Moreno
6 Ms Maria Nikolakaki / 85100 Rhodes / Greece / Nikitara 541
7 Excel Heights 501 / Edogawa-ku 139 / 7–3–8 Nakakasai / Japan / Tokyo /
   Mrs Junko Shiratori
8 301 Leighton Road / VHF Vehicles Ltd / London NW5 2QE /
   The Transport Director / Kentish Town

3   Letters: parts and layout

The parts of the letter below are in jumbled order. Write the numbers of the parts in the correct boxes in the letter plan, and label them with the terms in the box. The first one has been done for you.

| letterhead | date | inside address | salutation |
| body | complimentary close | signature block | enclosure |

2 letterhead

1 20 May 20—

2 **HALL & CO. LIMITED**
   BUILDERS' MERCHANTS
   Albert Road
   Peterborough
   PE2 7EK
   Tel: 01733 564231
   Fax: 01733 341865

   Email: mlongley@hallbuild.co.uk

3 Dear Mr Freeland

4 Mike Longley
   Sales Manager
   Hall & Co. Ltd

5 Yours sincerely

6 Enc.

7 Mr M. Freeland
   57 Coniston Crescent
   Dunstable
   Bedfordshire
   LU14 3RW

8 We note that you have made a planning
   application to extend your property, and I am
   writing to tell you about the building products
   and services which Hall & Co. provide.

   Our products start at the foundations with
   sand, cement, and bricks and we supply a full
   range of timber and plasterboard at unbeatable
   prices. We also offer a FREE ESTIMATING SERVICE
   with orders over £50.00.

   We feel sure you will find a lot to interest you
   in the enclosed brochure, and look forward to
   hearing from you.

4 Faxes and emails: true or false?

Read the following statements and decide which are true and which are false. Mark the true ones 'T' and the false ones 'F' in the spaces provided.

1 ☐ Confidential information should not be sent by fax and email.

2 ☐ If necessary, faxes can be used as substitutes for original documents.

3 ☐ *Fax* is a short form of the word *facts*.

4 ☐ Emails must end with *Yours faithfully* or *Yours sincerely*.

5 ☐ Emoticons can be added to business emails to make them look friendlier.

6 ☐ Using capital letters to write an email is the same as shouting.

7 ☐ @ in an email address means *automatic*.

8 ☐ A letter or card is usually more suitable than an email for a personal message.

9 ☐ In email header information, *c.c.* stands for *confidential copies*.

10 ☐ Emails are usually less formal than letters.

11 ☐ It is not as important to use correct grammar and spelling in a business email as it is in a letter.

12 ☐ The addressee's name comes after the @ sign in an email address.

5 Fax transmission form

Read this internal email from Yvonne Feltham, British Crystal's Export Manager, to her PA. Then complete the fax transmission form.

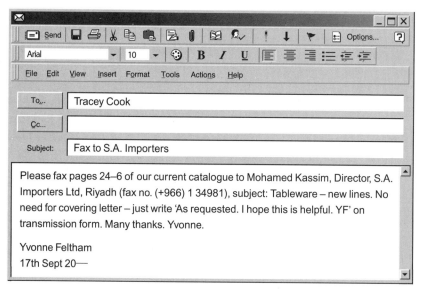

Please fax pages 24–6 of our current catalogue to Mohamed Kassim, Director, S.A. Importers Ltd, Riyadh (fax no. (+966) 1 34981), subject: Tableware – new lines. No need for covering letter – just write 'As requested. I hope this is helpful. YF' on transmission form. Many thanks. Yvonne.

Yvonne Feltham
17th Sept 20—

Fax

BRITISH CRYSTAL Ltd
Glazier House, Green Lane, Derby DE1 1RT

To: _____

From: _____

Fax no.: _____ Subject: _____

Date: _____ Page/s: _____

6 Email: request for further information

Mohamed Kassim has received Yvonne Feltham's fax. While he was reading the faxed catalogue he made notes about further information he needs. Read his notes and compose his email to Yvonne Feltham.

> *'York' range be available before end Oct?*
>
> *Approx. sales figures for 'Cambridge' range in other markets?*
>
> *'Bristol' range available in green? (can't read fax)*
>
> *'Durham' range – dishwasher-proof? (can't read fax)*

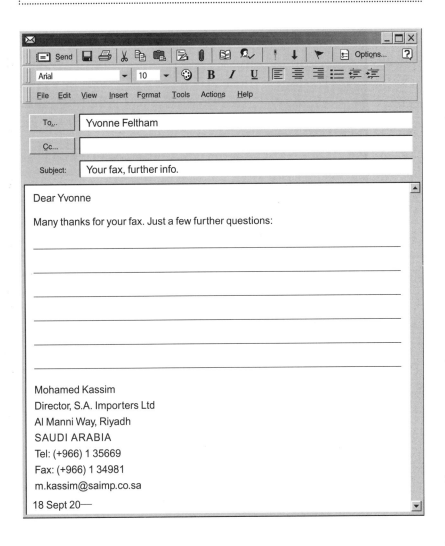

To... Yvonne Feltham

Cc...

Subject: Your fax, further info.

Dear Yvonne

Many thanks for your fax. Just a few further questions:

_____

_____

_____

_____

_____

_____

Mohamed Kassim
Director, S.A. Importers Ltd
Al Manni Way, Riyadh
SAUDI ARABIA
Tel: (+966) 1 35669
Fax: (+966) 1 34981
m.kassim@saimp.co.sa

18 Sept 20—

7 Email: checking

In this email, Terry Jordan, Manager of the Falcon Grange Hotel, is responding to an enquiry about conference facilities. If he sends it like this, he is in danger of losing a valuable customer – there are fourteen mistakes in it. Check the email, and correct the mistakes.

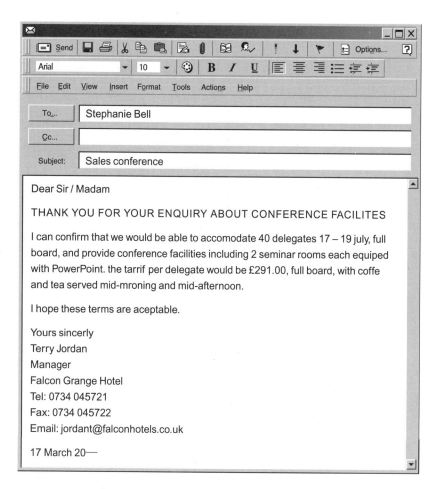

Dear Sir / Madam

THANK YOU FOR YOUR ENQUIRY ABOUT CONFERENCE FACILITES

I can confirm that we would be able to accomodate 40 delegates 17 – 19 july, full board, and provide conference facilities including 2 seminar rooms each equiped with PowerPoint. the tarrif per delegate would be £291.00, full board, with coffe and tea served mid-mroning and mid-afternoon.

I hope these terms are aceptable.

Yours sincerly
Terry Jordan
Manager
Falcon Grange Hotel
Tel: 0734 045721
Fax: 0734 045722
Email: jordant@falconhotels.co.uk

17 March 20—

8 Words and definitions

Make words from the jumbled letters and match them with the definitions below.

a LBCDEOK YSETL
b TERSGUANI CLOKB
c ERFCNEREE
d CSRULEENO

e EPITVAR NAD FIDNAILTCOEN
f BOJ TELTI
g SURYO ELERCISNY
h TTCMTHAEAN

1 Document enclosed with a letter.
2 Figures and / or letters written at the top of a letter to identify it.
3 Style of writing in which each line starts directly below the one above.
4 Complimentary close used at the end of a letter when the addressee's name is known.
5 Phrase written on a letter intended only to be read by the addressee.
6 Name and job title typed below a signature.
7 Separate document attached to an email message.
8 The name of someone's job, e.g. *Sales Manager, Chief Buyer*.

2
Content and style

1 Typical sentences

Sort out the jumbled words below to make six sentences typical of business correspondence. Add capital letters and punctuation as necessary.

1 grateful / soon / a / as / we / for / would / possible / reply / as / be
2 for / find / please / cheque / £49.50 / a / enclosed
3 further / please / if / us / information / you / any / contact / need
4 april / your / you / letter / thank / 5 / of / for
5 you / we / forward / to / from / look / hearing
6 pleasure / price list / enclosing / have / a / catalogue / our / I / spring / and / in

2 Courtesy

Rewrite the following request for payment in a more polite form.

Dear Sir

You have owed us £567.00 since February, which means you haven t paid us for three months.

We have written to you twice and you haven t bothered to answer us, yet you ve been a customer for years. Anyway, we re not going to put up with this, so if you don t tell us why you haven t paid, or send the money you owe us in ten days, we ll sue you. After all, we ve got bills to pay too, and besides we explained our rules for giving credit, i.e. payment on due dates, some time ago.

Yours, etc.

R. Lancaster (Mr)

3 Summarizing

Below is the reply to the letter in Exercise 2. It was opened by Mr Lancaster's secretary, who saw straight away that the letter is wordy and contains a lot of irrelevant information. Pretend you are the secretary and write Mr Lancaster an email summarizing the letter's contents. Try to make your summary no longer than seventy-five words.

Dear Mr Lancaster

I am writing to you in reply to your letter dated 9 May, which we received on 10 May, in which you reminded us of our outstanding balance, which now amounts to the sum total of £567.00.

I should like to offer my humblest apologies for our failure either to settle the account, or to reply to your two previous communications. However, I feel that I must explain the cause. We have been the unfortunate victims of a tragedy. Two months ago, our premises were almost completely destroyed by fire. Although I am happy to report that we sustained no casualties, all our records, stock, orders ready for despatch and so on, were consumed by the flames.

Now, at last, our fortunes are beginning to rise again, and our insurance company will shortly be releasing funds to facilitate our recovery. Let me assure you that you will be remunerated in full as soon as possible. In the interim, I would be grateful if you would accept a small sum towards the settlement of our account, with my personal promise that the remaining amount will be forwarded to you as soon as it becomes available.

Please find enclosed a cheque for the sum of £55.00, and once again, I beg you to accept my deepest apologies for any inconvenience caused.

Yours sincerely

T. D. Games (Mr)

4 Basing a letter on notes

Below is an email from Sarah Barnard, Sales Manager of Barnard Press, to Rosalind Wood, her secretary. Follow the instructions in the email, and write a letter of reply, setting it out in the spaces provided on the opposite page.

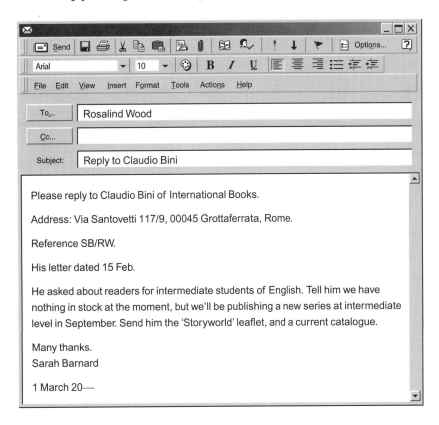

To... Rosalind Wood

Cc...

Subject: Reply to Claudio Bini

Please reply to Claudio Bini of International Books.

Address: Via Santovetti 117/9, 00045 Grottaferrata, Rome.

Reference SB/RW.

His letter dated 15 Feb.

He asked about readers for intermediate students of English. Tell him we have nothing in stock at the moment, but we'll be publishing a new series at intermediate level in September. Send him the 'Storyworld' leaflet, and a current catalogue.

Many thanks.
Sarah Barnard

1 March 20—

bp

Barnard Press Limited

183–7 Copwood Road
North Finchley
London N12 9PR
Telephone: +44 (0)20 8239 9653
Facsimile: +44 (0)20 8239 9754
Email: barnards@barnardpress.co.uk
www.barnardpress.co.uk

5 Clear sequence

This is a letter about arrangements for a business trip. At present it is difficult to understand because the ordering of the information is not clear. Rearrange the letter in a clearer sequence.

Dear Mr Jackson

NICOSIA COMPUTER TRAINING COURSE

I am writing with information about the arrangements we have made for your visit.

Unfortunately, Mr Charalambides will not be able to meet you in Larnaca on Thursday 15 June, as you requested, because he will be returning from a visit to our subsidiary in Spain. However, he will be back in the office the following day, so I have arranged for him to see you at 14.30.

On Friday 9 June your flight to Larnaca will be met by our driver, who will take you to the Amathus Beach Hotel, where we have booked you in for the first two nights. The driver will call for you at 17.00 on Sunday and drive you to the Training Centre at Nicosia. Most of the trainee operators will have had some experience of the new program by the time you arrive at the centre, but they will need a good deal of instruction on the more complex areas of the system.

We hope you enjoy your weekend at the hotel. The driver will pick you up from the Training Centre on Wednesday evening, at the end of the course, and take you back to the Amathus Beach Hotel, where I have booked you in for a further two nights.

Please could you confirm that you plan to return to London on the 18.30 flight on Friday 16, and also that the arrangements outlined here suit you?

Thank you for your letter of 18 May giving us the dates of your trip. I look forward to hearing from you.

Yours sincerely

Elena Theodorou

Training Manager

6 Planning

Mr Jackson is planning his reply to Ms Theodorou (see Exercise 5), using some rough notes he has made. Look at the notes and complete the plan below.

How many trainees on course? – London flight on 16 June leaves at 18.00, not 18.30. – Time of meeting with Charalambides OK - 9 June flight arrives Larnaca 15.30 – photocopying facilities at Training Centre?

paragraph 1   Acknowledge letter
paragraph 2   _____
paragraph 3   _____
paragraph 4   _____
paragraph 5   Thank Ms Theodorou for her help

Now, using your plan, write Mr Jackson's letter.

3
Enquiries

1 Enquiry from a building company

There are no capitals, punctuation, or paragraphs in this fax from a building company to a designer and manufacturer of kitchen units. Write out the fax correctly, dividing the body into four paragraphs.

Fax   **Clark Fitzpatrick Builders plc**
                                           Dunstable Road
                                           Luton, Bedfordshire
                                           LU2 3LM

To: ms doreen french
From: terry spalding household installations ltd
Fax no: 01582 351711
Subject: kitchen units
Date: 3 april 20—
Page/s: 2

dear ms french

thank you for your letter and the enclosed catalogue giving details of your kitchen units the main item we are interested in is the unit on page 22 it appears to meet all our specifications for the apartment block i described in my letter i am sending herewith a plan of a typical apartment which gives the exact dimensions before placing a firm order we would need samples of all materials used in the manufacture of the units could you please confirm that you guarantee all your products for two years against normal wear and tear i would also be grateful for details of your terms regarding payment and of any trade and quantity discounts if the price and quality of your products are satisfactory we will place further orders as we have several projects at the planning stage

yours sincerely

terry spalding

purchasing manager

---

2 Words and definitions

Make words from the jumbled letters and match them with the definitions below.

a UEAGTOCLA   e LAOEEHSLWR   i ELSA RO ETRRNU
b METIESAT   f WOSORHOM   j NATYUTQI DSNUOTCI
c ERENTD   g IDISYUSRAB
d ETSMCOUR   h POSSUTCREP

1 Company that is partly owned by a larger one.
2 Person who buys goods or services from a shop or company.
3 Money taken off the usual selling price of goods when the buyer is purchasing a large amount.
4 Place where a company demonstrates its products.
5 Publication giving details of goods or services offered by a company.
6 Price given for work to be done.
7 Written estimate, usually for a large job such as building a factory.
8 Publication giving details about a school or college.
9 Person or company that buys goods from manufacturers and sells them to retailers.
10 Term used when a supplier agrees to buy back unsold goods.

3 Polite requests

John Phillips is telling his PA to write various letters. Change his instructions into an acceptable form for business correspondence. Each sentence has been started for you.

EXAMPLE John Phillips: 'Ask them for a cash discount.' *Could you...*
PA writes: *Could you offer us a cash discount?*

1 'Tell Rockfords that the consignment must be delivered before the end of September.'
   It is essential _____

2 'Ask Schmidt to send us their catalogue and a price list.'
   Could you _____

3 'We're going to give them a big order, so find out if they allow quantity discounts.'
   As we intend to place a substantial _____

4 'If they can't deliver the goods before Friday, tell Larousse to email us.'
   Please could you _____

5 'It would be a lot of help if they could send some samples.'
   We would appreciate _____

6 'Say that we'd like Andover to send someone here to give us an estimate.'
   We would be grateful if _____

7 'Say we'd like to see a demonstration of both models.'
   We would be interested _____

8 'Find out if Weston's will let us have twenty units on approval.'
   Would you be _____

9 'Ask when he will let us have the cheque.'
   I am writing to enquire _____

10 'Say our suppliers generally let us settle by monthly statement.'
   As a rule _____

4 Enquiry to a college

Complete this letter of enquiry to a college with the prepositions from the box.

in (×4) for (×2) to by with at of (×2)

Avda. San Antonio 501
80260 Bellaterra
Barcelona
Spain

12 October 20—

Admissions Department
International College
145–8 Regents Road
Falmer
Brighton BN1 9QN

Dear Sir / Madam

I am a single 23 year-old Spanish student **1**_____ the
University **2**_____ Barcelona doing a Master s Course
3_____ Business Studies, and I intend to spend six
months **4**_____ England, beginning **5**_____ January next
year, preparing **6**_____ the Cambridge First
Certificate.

Your college was recommended **7**_____ me **8**_____
a fellow student and I would like details **9**_____ your
First Certificate courses, including fees and dates.
Could you also let me know if you can provide
accommodation **10**_____ me **11**_____ Brighton **12**_____
an English family?

Thank you for your attention, and I look forward to
hearing from you soon.

Yours faithfully

María Ortega

5 An application form

International College have replied to Maria Ortega's letter of enquiry (see Exercise 4) and enclosed an application form. Imagine that you are Maria. You have decided to take the First Certificate course starting on 3 January and finishing on 26 June 20— . You are paying the fees yourself, and today's date is 10 November 20— . Complete the form using the information here and in Maria's letter.

Student Application Form

International College • 145–8 Regents Road • Falmer • Brighton • BN1 9QN

APPLICANT

Family Name: _____

Other Names: _____

Title Mr / Mrs / Miss / Ms: _____   Age: _____

Address: _____

_____

Town / city: _____   Country: _____

Do you have a job or are you a student? _____

Job title / Subject of study: _____

Name of business / university / college: _____

Course applied for: _____

Course dates: _____

Are you paying your own fees, or is your company paying for you?

_____

Will you find your own accommodation or do you want this to be arranged by the College? _____

Please tick how you found out about International College.

☐ Newspaper   ☐ Friend's recommendation

☐ Through your university / college   ☐ Other source: _____

Signature: _____   Date: _____

6 Enquiry from a retailer   Write the letter of enquiry to which the letter below is a reply. You are M. Morreau, and you saw an advertisement for Glaston Potteries' latest designs for oven-to-table ware in the May edition of *International Homes*.

GLASTON POTTERIES LTD

Clayfield | Burnley | BB10 1RQ

Telephone + 44 (0)1282 46125
Facsimile + 44 (0)1282 63182
Email j.merton@glaston.co.uk
www.glaston.com

Your ref: JFM/PS

2 July 20—

M. J.F. Morreau
Director
Cuisines Morreau S.A.
1150 boulevard Calbert
F—54015 Nancy Cedex

Dear M. Morreau

Thank you for your enquiry of 28 June in which you expressed an interest in retailing a selection of our products in your shops in Nancy.

Please find enclosed our current catalogue and price list. You might also be interested in visiting our website.

In response to your request for a 20% trade discount, we regret that we cannot offer more than 15%. However, we do give a 5% quantity discount on orders over €20,000. In comparison with similar companies in the UK, these terms are extremely competitive. Payment would need to be by sight draft until we have established a business relationship.

Finally, we are confident that we can deliver well within the two-month time limit you require.

Thank you for your interest. We hope to hear from you soon.

Yours sincerely

J. Merton

Sales Manager

Enc.

Registered No. 716481
VAT Registered No. 133 53431 08

4
Replies and quotations

1 Reply to an enquiry

Mr Chan has emailed Hübner GmbH, enquiring about some earth-moving equipment he saw at a trade fair. In his reply, Hübner's Sales Director, Gustav Fest, refers to specific questions asked by Mr Chan. Read Herr Fest's email and tick the items which Mr Chan asked about.

1 ☐ How soon the goods can be delivered
2 ☐ Details of prices
3 ☐ Where the goods can be purchased
4 ☐ After-sales service
5 ☐ How the goods will be transported
6 ☐ Terms of payment
7 ☐ Quantity discounts
8 ☐ Cash discounts
9 ☐ Details of the range of goods available
10 ☐ Which bank will handle the transaction
11 ☐ Guarantees

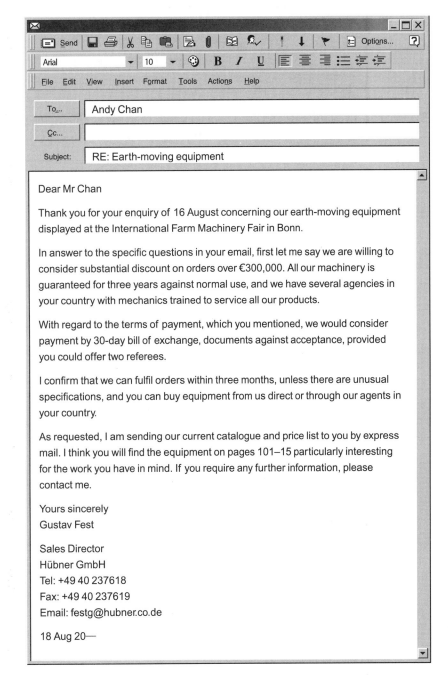

Send | Options... | ?

Arial | 10 | B *I* U

File Edit View Insert Format Tools Actions Help

To... Andy Chan
Cc...
Subject: RE: Earth-moving equipment

Dear Mr Chan

Thank you for your enquiry of 16 August concerning our earth-moving equipment displayed at the International Farm Machinery Fair in Bonn.

In answer to the specific questions in your email, first let me say we are willing to consider substantial discount on orders over €300,000. All our machinery is guaranteed for three years against normal use, and we have several agencies in your country with mechanics trained to service all our products.

With regard to the terms of payment, which you mentioned, we would consider payment by 30-day bill of exchange, documents against acceptance, provided you could offer two referees.

I confirm that we can fulfil orders within three months, unless there are unusual specifications, and you can buy equipment from us direct or through our agents in your country.

As requested, I am sending our current catalogue and price list to you by express mail. I think you will find the equipment on pages 101–15 particularly interesting for the work you have in mind. If you require any further information, please contact me.

Yours sincerely
Gustav Fest

Sales Director
Hübner GmbH
Tel: +49 40 237618
Fax: +49 40 237619
Email: festg@hubner.co.de

18 Aug 20—

2 Question forms

Here are some of the questions Mr Chan asked (see Exercise 1), but the words have been mixed up. Rearrange the words so that the questions makes sense and add the necessary capitals and punctuation.

EXAMPLE   offer / do / you / large / a / orders / discount / on
Do you offer a discount on large orders?

1 details / of / can / you / prices / please / me / send / your
2 after-sales / do / an / offer / you / service
3 guaranteed / are / for / how / goods / long / the
4 goods / can / how / delivered / soon / the / be
5 terms / what / payment / your / of / are
6 can / buy / where / the / I / goods
7 you / do / what / quantity / discounts / sort / offer / of
8 can / send / mail / please / your / by / me / you / express / catalogue

3 Words and definitions

Make words from the jumbled letters and match them with the definitions below.

a TMINEROC
b TEN RCIPE
c RIGACREA ROFDRAW
d TNQOAOIUT
e NREDU PATESRAE VREOC
f SORSG IERPC
g LTAYOLY NUTCOSID

1 Condition of sale when the customer pays for the transport of the goods.
2 Internationally used term which indicates which price is being quoted to the customer.
3 Price which does not include additional costs such as transport and insurance.
4 Amount taken off the usual price of goods when they are sold to a regular customer.
5 In a separate envelope or parcel.
6 Price which includes additional costs such as transport and insurance.
7 Price for work to be done or a service to be provided.

4 Reply to a request for information (1)

There are no capitals or paragraphs in this reply to a request for information. Write it out correctly, adding the capitals, and dividing the body of the letter into four paragraphs.

```
dear mr russell

thank you for your phone call of thursday 4 march enquiring
about hiring our delivery vans. my colleague ms angela
smith, who took the call, said you were mainly interested in
5-ton vehicles like the 'tobor' so i am enclosing our booklet
'small truck hire' giving you details of our charges. these
also appear on our website at www.vanhire.co.uk. you will
notice that the summer months of june, july and august are
the least expensive and that we offer a 20 per cent discount
on weekend hire starting saturday at 08.00 and ending sunday
at 20.00. our main offices in the uk are in london and
birmingham, but we also have branches in france, germany,
and italy. if you are thinking of hiring abroad you will
find details on our website. please let me know if i can be
of further help.

yours sincerely
michael craddock
transport manager
van hire unlimited
```

5 Incoterms

Incoterms indicate which price the seller is quoting to the customer, for example DAF (Delivered at frontier) means that the seller pays all delivery costs to the buyer's frontier, but not import duty. In the table below, the explanations have become confused. Match the correct Incoterm to its explanation.

Incoterm	Explanation
1 DDU (delivery duty unpaid)	a The buyer pays all delivery costs once the goods have left the seller's factory or warehouse.
2 CFR (cost and freight)	b The seller pays all delivery costs to the port.
3 CIF (cost, insurance, and freight)	c The seller pays all delivery costs, except for import duty, to a named destination.
4 EXW (ex-works)	d The seller pays all delivery costs to a named destination, except for insurance.
5 FAS (free alongside ship)	e The seller pays all delivery costs to when the goods are on board ship.
6 FOB (free on board)	f The seller pays all delivery costs to a named destination.

6 Reply to a request for information (2)

Read this email from Gerd Busch, Marketing Manager of Busch AG, to his PA. Imagine you are the PA and use the information he gives to write a letter replying to Anne Croft of Shape-up Fitness Centres on Herr Busch's behalf.

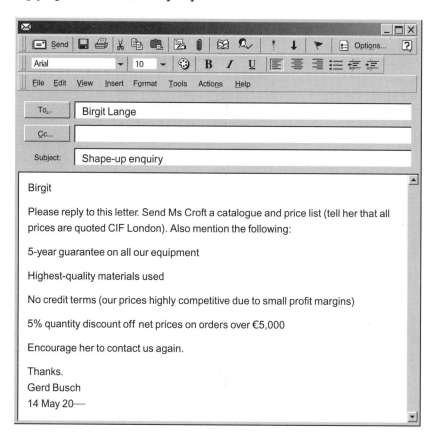

To... Birgit Lange

Cc...

Subject: Shape-up enquiry

Birgit

Please reply to this letter. Send Ms Croft a catalogue and price list (tell her that all prices are quoted CIF London). Also mention the following:

5-year guarantee on all our equipment

Highest-quality materials used

No credit terms (our prices highly competitive due to small profit margins)

5% quantity discount off net prices on orders over €5,000

Encourage her to contact us again.

Thanks.
Gerd Busch
14 May 20—

7 An estimate

Steve Smart, of MG Heating Engineers, is telling his secretary to send a customer, Mr Frost, an estimate. As Steve Smart's secretary, write Mr Frost a letter based on the instructions below. Set out the prices in tabulated form, including both subtotal and total with VAT.

'And please send Mr Frost an estimate for upgrading the central heating system in his offices. Thank him for his phone call and tell him that we can fit the seven thermostatic valves at £20 per valve – and the lockshield valve would also cost £20. Drawing down the system before we do the fitting is £40, and filling and balancing it afterwards is £50. Oh, and add VAT at 17.5% to all that. Tell him that we can do it before the end of September, but if he wants it done over a weekend he'll have to pay an additional £80.00 for overtime ... and don't forget to say that all prices quoted include materials and labour. Oh yes – and tell him to contact me if he has any more questions.'

5
Orders

1 Verbs used with *order*

The verbs in the box can all be used with the noun 'order'. Choose the best verb to complete each sentence. Use each verb only once, and in the correct form.

confirm	refuse	ship	despatch
place	make up	cancel	acknowledge

1 We would like to _____ an order with you for 5,000 units.

2 As we are unable to supply the quantity you asked for, we would have no objection if you preferred to _____ your order.

3 I am writing to _____ your order, which we received this morning, for 20 'Omega Engines'.

4 We are pleased to inform you that your order K451 has already been _____ from our depot.

5 Please _____ your order in writing, so that we can inform our distribution depot.

6 Your order was _____ yesterday on the MV *Oxford*.

7 Unfortunately, we shall have to _____ your order unless payment is settled in cash.

8 I would like to reassure you that your order will be _____ in our depot by staff who have experience in handling these delicate materials.

2 Placing an order: accompanying email

In this email Mr Takahashi is placing an order, but the sentences have become confused. Rewrite the email with the sentences in the correct order, starting new paragraphs where appropriate.

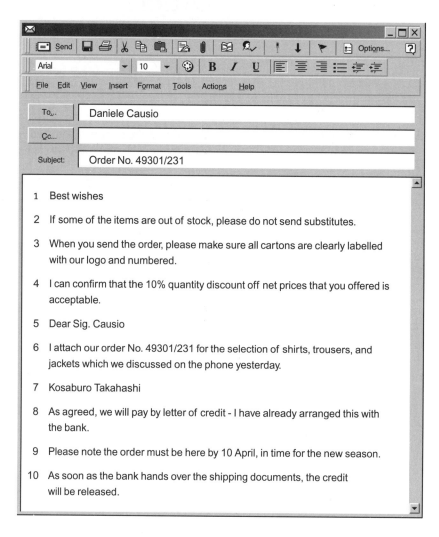

To... Daniele Causio

Cc...

Subject: Order No. 49301/231

1 Best wishes

2 If some of the items are out of stock, please do not send substitutes.

3 When you send the order, please make sure all cartons are clearly labelled with our logo and numbered.

4 I can confirm that the 10% quantity discount off net prices that you offered is acceptable.

5 Dear Sig. Causio

6 I attach our order No. 49301/231 for the selection of shirts, trousers, and jackets which we discussed on the phone yesterday.

7 Kosaburo Takahashi

8 As agreed, we will pay by letter of credit - I have already arranged this with the bank.

9 Please note the order must be here by 10 April, in time for the new season.

10 As soon as the bank hands over the shipping documents, the credit will be released.

3 Order form

Read this email from Dieter Faust, a buying manager, to his assistant, Beatrice Mey.

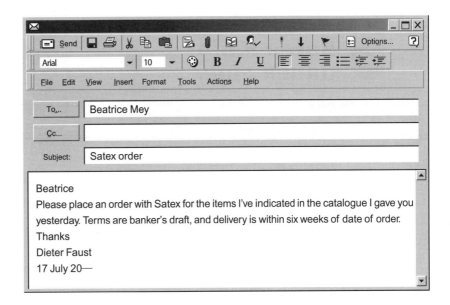

Here is the page from the sales catalogue Dieter Faust mentioned in his email.

Satex S.p.A.
SPRING CATALOGUE

Item		Cat. no.	Price € per item	Quantity
Shirts				
PLAIN	white	S288	€30	50
	blue	S289	€30	50
STRIPED	blue / white	S301	€35	
	white / grey	S302	€35	
	white / green	S303	€35	
Sweaters (V-neck)				
PLAIN	red	P112	€40	20
	blue	P113	€40	20
	black	P114	€40	
PATTERNED	blue	P305	€52	
	black	P306	€52	

As Beatrice Mey, use the information in his email and the catalogue to complete this order form.

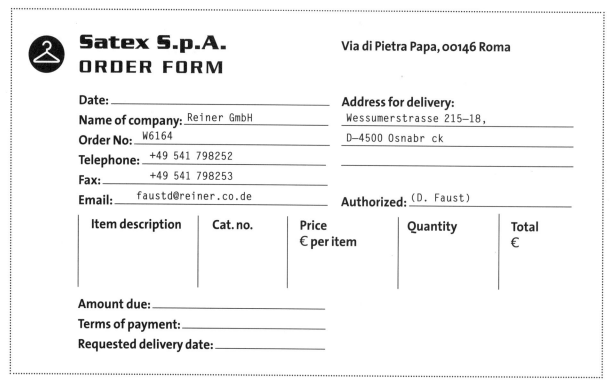

Satex S.p.A.
ORDER FORM

Via di Pietra Papa, 00146 Roma

Date: _____

Name of company: Reiner GmbH

Order No: W6164

Telephone: +49 541 798252

Fax: +49 541 798253

Email: faustd@reiner.co.de

Address for delivery:
Wessumerstrasse 215–18,

D–4500 Osnabr ck

Authorized: (D. Faust)

Item description	Cat. no.	Price € per item	Quantity	Total €

Amount due: _____

Terms of payment: _____

Requested delivery date: _____

4 Placing an order: covering letter

Dieter Faust emails Beatrice Mey again, reminding her to include a covering letter with the Satex order (see Exercise 3). As she has only recently started working for him, he gives detailed instructions. As Beatrice Mey, write the letter.

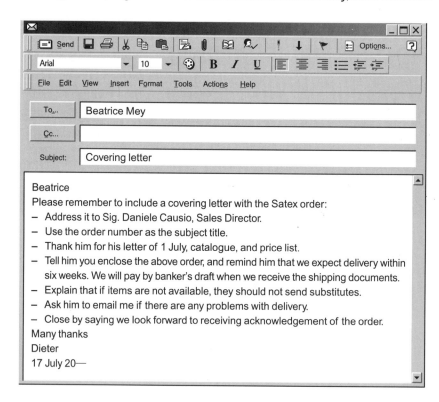

To... Beatrice Mey

Cc...

Subject: Covering letter

Beatrice
Please remember to include a covering letter with the Satex order:
— Address it to Sig. Daniele Causio, Sales Director.
— Use the order number as the subject title.
— Thank him for his letter of 1 July, catalogue, and price list.
— Tell him you enclose the above order, and remind him that we expect delivery within six weeks. We will pay by banker's draft when we receive the shipping documents.
— Explain that if items are not available, they should not send substitutes.
— Ask him to email me if there are any problems with delivery.
— Close by saying we look forward to receiving acknowledgement of the order.
Many thanks
Dieter
17 July 20—

5 Acknowledging an order

There are no capitals, punctuation, or paragraphs in this email acknowledging an order. Write it out correctly. Divide the body of the email into two paragraphs.

To... Georges Delmas

Cc...

Subject: Your order No. R497

dear m delmas

thank you for your order (no r497) which we are at present making up the instruments will be packed individually in 8 crates numbered and marked with our logo they will be sent airfreight cif marseille to reach you no later than 18 may our invoice showing the 12% trade and 3% quantity discounts the insurance certificate and the air waybill will be sent to the bank of marseille as requested

harald kjaer
sales manager
dansk industries, kongens nytorv 1, dk–1050 københavn k
tel: +45 367521
fax: +45 367522
email: hkjaer@dansk.co.de
7 may 20—

6 Delay in delivery

Read this extract from a fax apologizing for a delayed delivery, and choose the best words from the options in brackets.

Further to our telephone conversation on Friday, I am writing to you

1 _____ (affecting, concerning, changing) your order, No. SX1940,

which was **2** _____ (sold, made, placed) with us on 10 January.

Once again, I must **3** _____ (regret, apologize, speak) for

the delay in processing this order. This was due to a staffing

4 _____ (shortage, fault, malfunction). However, since I spoke to you,

we have **5** _____ (dismissed, promoted, taken on) four new

employees at our depot, and I am pleased to tell you that your order is now ready

for despatch. It will **6** _____ (arrive, deliver, reach) you within five

working days.

Special **7** _____ (care, attention, caution) has been taken to ensure

that the **8** _____ (load, crates, consignment) has been packed

9 _____ (meeting, according, serving) to your requirements. Each

item will be individually wrapped to **10** _____ (prevent, cause, stop) damage.

7 Refusing an order

All the sentences below give reasons for refusing an order. Match the sentences in column A with sentences in column B with similar meanings. Then put a tick by the sentences which are most suitable for business correspondence.

Column A

1 We don't make this product now because people don't buy enough of it.

2 We can't sell you anything unless you pay cash.

3 We cannot offer the discount you suggest as our profit margins are extremely low.

4 We can't possibly fill this huge order: it's more than our total output for at least six months!

5 Unfortunately, we cannot guarantee delivery within five working days.

Column B

a Unfortunately, we do not have the capacity to supply an order as large as this.

b We can't let you have 15% off because we price our products as cheaply as possible.

c There's no way we can deliver in such a short time.

d We have stopped manufacturing this product as there is no longer sufficient demand.

e We regret that we would only be prepared to supply on a cash basis.

8 Words and definitions

Make words from the jumbled letters and match them with the definitions below.

a SMPOMILCTEN IPLS
b NOVCIIE
c GIFOWRDNRA GNETA
d TSTMTEELEN
e RIA ILWYALB
f IHPS
g VIGCNERO TRTEEL
h CIAVDE TNEO

1 Person or organization that conveys goods to their destination.
2 Letter accompanying a document or goods, explaining the contents.
3 List of goods or services that states how much must be paid for them.
4 Document informing a customer that a consignment is on its way to them.
5 Payment of an account.
6 Small piece of paper with a company's details on it.
7 To send goods by road, rail, air, or sea.
8 Document that gives information about goods sent by air.

6
Payment

1 Invoice

M. Morreau has ordered the following dinner services from Glaston Potteries: ten 'Lotus' at £35 each, catalogue number L305; twenty 'Wedgwood' at £43 each, catalogue number W218. Cost, insurance, and freight are included in these prices. Glaston have offered him a 15% trade discount. Complete the invoice below.

GLASTON POTTERIES LTD

Clayfield | Burnley | BB10 1RQ

Telephone + 44 (0)1282 46125
Facsimile + 44 (0)1282 63182
Email accounts@glaston.co.uk
www.glaston.com

J. F. Morreau
1150 boulevard Calbert
F–54015 Nancy Cedex

9 May 20—

Your order No. 3716

Quantity	Description	Cat. No.	£ each	£
_____	_____	_____	_____	_____
_____	_____	_____	_____	_____
_____	_____	_____	_____	_____
_____	_____	_____	_____	_____

CIF_____   _____

Less _____ discount off net price _____

                    Total _____

Payment due within 28 days of date of invoice.

E&OE

Registered No. 716481
VAT Reg. No. 133 53431 08

2 Statement of account

You work in the Accounts Department of Homemakers Ltd, a furniture manufacturer, and are preparing a monthly statement for a regular customer, R. Hughes & Son Ltd. Your first entry is the Account Rendered, i.e. the outstanding balance of £461.00 from last month, which goes in the Balance column. This column also shows a running balance of all the other items. All the money Hughes owes you, including the debit note, goes in the Debit column. All the money he has paid, including the credit note, goes in the Credit column. Complete the May statement using the information below.

Customer: R. Hughes & Son Ltd, 21 Mead Road, Swansea, West Glamorgan 3ST 1DR

Date	Item	Amount
1 May	Account Rendered	£461.00
5 May	Invoice 771/2	£781.00
7 May	Cheque	£300.00
12 May	C/N 216	£285.00
16 May	Invoice 824/2	£302.00
18 May	Cheque	£200.00
23 May	D/N 306	£100.00

The terms at the end of the statement are a Cash Discount of 3% if the statement is paid within 10 days.

HOMEMAKERS

54–59 Riverside, Cardiff CF1 1JW
Telephone: +44 (0)29 20 49721
Fax: +44 (0)29 20 49937

statement

To: _____

Date	Item	Debit	Credit	Balance
1 May	Account Rendered			
Terms:				

3 Request for more time to settle an account

M. Morreau received the consignment from Glaston Potteries (see Exercise 1). Unfortunately he is unable to pay within the period stated on Glaston's invoice. He writes to John Merton, Sales Manager at Glaston, to apologize. Rewrite his letter in less elaborate language: leave out any details which are not relevant.

Dear Mr Merton

I deeply regret that at this moment in time I am unable to settle your invoice dated 9 May for my order No. 3716 for ten Lotus dinner services at £35 each, catalogue number L305, and twenty 'Wedgwood' dinner services at £43 each, catalogue number W218.

The consignment arrived in good condition and as usual I admired the quality and elegance of your products. They always sell very well in my two shops here in Nancy. Unfortunately, two days after the arrival of the consignment, disaster struck. After several centimetres of incessant rain my stockroom was completely flooded and much of the stock damaged or destroyed.

I am waiting with great patience for my insurers to settle my claim, but meanwhile it is with sorrow that I have to tell you that I am unable to pay any of my suppliers. However, on a more optimistic note, I am able to inform you that the aforementioned insurers have promised me compensation within the next four weeks. When I receive this, I will take measures to pay all my suppliers as soon as I possibly can.

Trusting that you will understand this difficult situation, I remain

Your humble servant

Jean Morreau (M.)

4 Crossword

Complete the crossword

ACROSS

1 A _____ note is a form of IOU (*I owe you*).

2 If your supplier has charged too much on an invoice, ask for a _____ .

3 An _____ lists goods or services, and how much must be paid for them.

4 An international money _____ can be bought at the bank to settle an account in another country.

5 A bank _____ is a cheque that a bank draws on itself and sells to a customer.

6 After two requests for payment you might receive a final _____ .

7 _____ is a system for transferring money from one bank or post office to another.

DOWN

8 A _____ _____ invoice is sent in advance of the goods ordered. (2 words: 3, 5)

9 A customer can request a bank to _____ money from one account to another.

5 Request for payment

Choose the best words from the options in brackets in this letter requesting payment.

 **UK Cycles Ltd**

Borough House Borough Road Cleveland TS1 3BA

Telephone: +44 (0)191 572954
Fax: +44 (0)191 572595
Email: accounts@ukcycles.co.uk
www.ukcycles.co.uk

28 April 20—

Karl Janssen
Managing Director
Velo Sport AG
Karlstr. 45
D–5230 Sömmerda

Account No. VS 301632

Dear Mr Janssen

We wrote to you on 25 March concerning the above **1**_____ (*account, bill*) for £2,700.00 which has now been outstanding **2**_____ (*for, since, about*) three months. When we agreed to offer you credit facilities we pointed out that it was essential to **3**_____ (*pay, clear, handle*) accounts **4**_____ (*in, at, on*) the exact date, particularly as we generally do not **5**_____ (*supply, present, offer*) credit terms.

As you realize, delayed payments can create problems for us **6**_____ (*by, to, with*) our own suppliers, therefore we would appreciate it if you could either let us know why the **7**_____ (*balance, credit, payment*) has not been paid, or let us have a remittance **8**_____ (*within, for, during*) the next ten days.

We would be grateful if this could receive your immediate attention.

Yours sincerely

Helen Stuart (MS)

Chief Accountant

6 Reply to request for payment

Karl Janssen emails his PA, Renata Heynold, asking her to draft a reply to Helen Stuart (see Exercise 5). As Renata Heynold, write the reply.

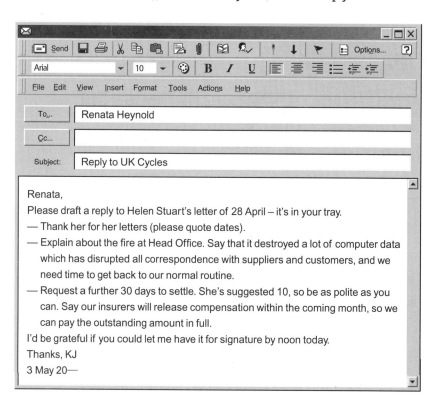

Renata,

Please draft a reply to Helen Stuart's letter of 28 April – it's in your tray.

— Thank her for her letters (please quote dates).

— Explain about the fire at Head Office. Say that it destroyed a lot of computer data which has disrupted all correspondence with suppliers and customers, and we need time to get back to our normal routine.

— Request a further 30 days to settle. She's suggested 10, so be as polite as you can. Say our insurers will release compensation within the coming month, so we can pay the outstanding amount in full.

I'd be grateful if you could let me have it for signature by noon today.

Thanks, KJ

3 May 20—

7 Formal and informal English

Match the sentences in column A with sentences in column B with similar meanings. One sentence in each pair is in formal English (i.e. appropriate for business correspondence), and the other is informal. Write 'F' beside the formal sentences and 'I' beside the informal ones.

Column A

1 ☐ We expect to receive your remittance within seven days.

2 ☐ We are taking you to court to get our money back.

3 ☐ I apologize for not clearing the balance earlier.

4 ☐ It appears that this invoice has not yet been settled.

5 ☐ We would be grateful for another month to settle.

Column B

a ☐ We want you to pay us in less than a week.

b ☐ Sorry I didn't pay you before now.

c ☐ We can't pay you in less than four weeks.

d ☐ Unfortunately, we have no alternative but to take legal action to recover the debt.

e ☐ It looks as though you haven't paid us yet.

8 Words and definitions

Make words from the jumbled letters and match them with the definitions below.

a RTURECN CNATCUO
b HISGT FADTR
c NLACEBA
d KANB NARRSEFT
e TDCRYAMUONE IDERCT
f EUD TAED
g SETTORP
h EMTACNEITR
i EMATTESTN FO TANCOCU
j BEDTI TENO

1 Take legal action to obtain payment.
2 Date by which an account should be settled.
3 Account into which a customer can pay money, or draw it out, without giving notice.
4 Movement of money from one bank account to another.
5 Payment.
6 Difference between the totals of money coming into and going out of a bank account.
7 List of amounts paid and owed.
8 Document informing a customer of money owed.
9 Bill of exchange that must be paid immediately it is presented.
10 Letter of credit that requires the seller to supply shipping documents to the bank to obtain payment.

7
Complaints and adjustments

1 Formal and informal English

All the sentences below could be used in complaints, or replies to them. Match the sentences in column A with sentences in column B with similar meanings. Then put a tick by the sentences which are most suitable for business correspondence.

Column A

1 You should put it right.
2 Please ensure that the problem does not arise again.
3 In this case we are not responsible for the error.
4 Please could you send us a refund.
5 We're sorry about the muddle.
6 We're planning to buy from someone else.
7 Your machine doesn't work.
8 I regret that in this case we are unwilling to offer a refund.

Column B

a We want our money back.
b We would be grateful if you could correct the error.
c We apologize for the confusion.
d We will have to consider changing to another supplier.
e There appears to be a defect in the mechanism.
f We're not giving you your money back.
g This time it's not our fault.
h Make sure it doesn't happen again.

2 Complaint about damage

Complete this letter of complaint about damage with the words and expressions from the box.

wear	crates	rusty
insurers	inspecting	consignment
complain	refund	handled
torn	invoice	carriage forward

C. R. Méndez S.A.

Avda. del Ejército 83
E–48015
Bilbao
Tel: +34 94 231907
Fax: +34 94 245618
Email: mendezc@crmendez.co.es

15 October 20—

Mr B. Harrison
Sales Manager
Seymore Furniture Ltd
Tib Street
Maidenhead
Berks SL6 5DS

Dear Mr Harrison

I am writing to **1**_____ about a shipment of tubular steel garden furniture we received yesterday against **2**_____ No. G 3190/1.

The **3**_____ were damaged on the outside, and looked as if they had been roughly **4**_____. When we unpacked them, we found that some of the chair legs were bent and **5**_____, and the fabric on the seating **6**_____, or showing signs of **7**_____.

Two further crates from the **8**_____ have not arrived yet, so we have not had the opportunity of **9**_____ them. I have told the shipping company that we cannot accept this consignment from you, and they have contacted your **10**_____.

As we will be unable to retail this consignment in our stores, we are returning the shipment to you **11**_____, and we shall expect a full **12**_____.

Yours sincerely

C. R. Méndez

Managing Director

---

3 Complaint about late delivery

There are no capitals, punctuation, or paragraphs in this letter of complaint about late delivery to a manufacturer of medical equipment. Write out the letter correctly. Divide the body of the letter into two paragraphs.

ISTITUTO DI MEDICINA Viale Bracci
1–61001 Siena
Telefono: +39 0586 43-74-25
Fax: +39 0586 43-74-26
Email: clotti@imed.ac.it

15 june 20—

mr h. toda
sales manager
nihon instruments
12–18 wakakusa-cho
hagashi-osaka-shi
osaka-fu
japan

dear mr toda

awb 4156/82

we are writing to point out that the above delivery which arrived yesterday was a week late this is the second time we have had to write to you on this subject and we cannot allow the situation to continue we have already explained that it is essential for medical equipment to arrive on due dates as late delivery could create a very serious problem unless we have your firm guarantee on the promptness of all future deliveries we will have to look for another supplier please could you confirm this before we place our next order

yours sincerely

carlo lotti (sig.)

head of administration

4 Reply to complaint about damage

Brian Harrison, Sales Manager at Seymore Furniture, emails Jo Hayes, his PA, asking her to draft a reply to Sr Méndez (see Exercise 2). Note that his instructions only concern the letter's content and signature: he assumes that Jo will open and close it in an appropriate way. As Jo Hayes, write the letter.

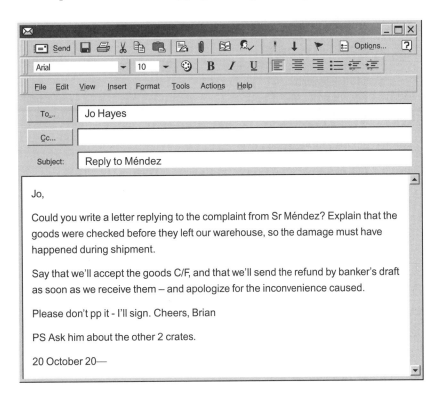

5 Reply to complaint about late delivery

The sentences have become confused in Mr Toda's reply to Sig. Lotti's letter (see Exercise 3). Rewrite the letter with the sentences in the correct order, starting new paragraphs where appropriate.

1 **Consignment no. AWB 4156/82**
2 I trust that this will clarify the situation, and look forward to continued good trading with you.
3 However, the two orders you mentioned were sent to our factory rather than our administrative offices at the above address.
4 We would like to take this opportunity of reminding you that to avoid delay in future all orders should be sent to our office address.
5 Sales Manager
6 Thank you for your letter of 15 June concerning late delivery of the above consignment.
7 Hirio Toda (Mr)
8 We understand how important prompt deliveries are to our customers.
9 Dear Mr Lotti
10 Yours sincerely

6 Complaint about accounting errors

You work for IT Services plc, King Street, London w8 2mc. Excel Stationers supply your company with stationery. They have sent you the invoice below. The wrong totals have been given for three of the items, which of course results in an incorrect final total.

1 Find the mistakes and work out the correct figures.
2 Write to Excel Stationers. Your contact is Mrs B. Grevon, Accounts Department.
   — Say what the mistakes are and what the correct version should be.
   — Tell her that you will settle the account when you receive a corrected invoice.
   — Mention that this has happened several times before, and that you will change your suppliers if it happens again.

Excel Stationers Ltd
28 Langley Estate
Templetown
London WC3 7AL

☎ +44 (0)20 7192 9880
🖶 +44 (0)20 7192 9437

Invoice No. 3910

20 November 20—

IT Services plc
King Street
London W8 2MC

Quantity	Item/s	Price	Total £
12	Writing pads each @	2.80	35.30
8	Packets window envelopes each @	2.20	17.60
3	Boxes 'Stylo' Pens each @	1.50	3.50
8	Reams multi-purpose paper each @	3.90	33.20
		TOTAL	**89.60**

8
Credit

1 Formal and informal English

In the sentences below, the words in italics are not very appropriate for formal correspondence. Choose a more suitable alternative from the box.

inform	overdue	request	promptly	sufficient
elapsed	acceptable	competitive	settle	confidential

1 Thank you for forwarding the documents so *quickly*.
2 We feel that *enough* time has *passed* for you to *pay*.
3 I am writing to *ask for* open account facilities.
4 We would like to remind you that this information is highly *secret*.
5 Your quarterly settlement is three weeks *late*.
6 We are pleased to *tell* you that the credit facilities you asked for are *fine*.
7 Our prices are very *low*.

2 Agreeing to credit

As Alex Rempel, Sales Manager of Rempel GmbH, reply to the email below from Thomas Shaw. Agree to his request for credit, but tell him, politely, that according to your records the period for settlement was 30 days, not 60. Apologize for any misunderstanding. Ask him to confirm that these terms are acceptable and say that, if they are, he will not need to provide references.

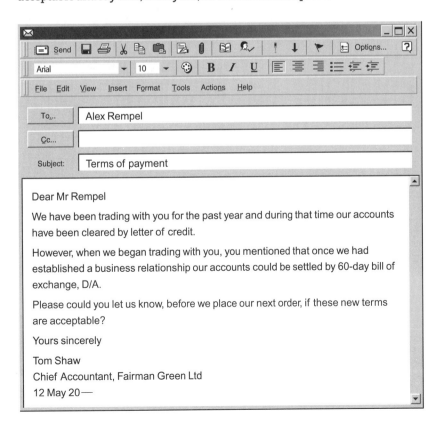

Dear Mr Rempel

We have been trading with you for the past year and during that time our accounts have been cleared by letter of credit.

However, when we began trading with you, you mentioned that once we had established a business relationship our accounts could be settled by 60-day bill of exchange, D/A.

Please could you let us know, before we place our next order, if these new terms are acceptable?

Yours sincerely

Tom Shaw
Chief Accountant, Fairman Green Ltd
12 May 20—

3 Request for a reference   Complete the following request for a reference with the correct prepositions.

Antonio Medina S.L.

C/Sagasta 1156
Barcelona 08317
Teléfono: +34 93 478503
Fax: +34 93 479152
Email: pgomez@medina.co.es

18 May 20—

Mr Gerald MacFee
Credit Controller
British Suppliers plc
Hoxteth House
Wrights Way
Glasgow G12 8QQ

Dear Mr MacFee

We are writing **1**_____ you **2**_____ the recommendation
3_____ Mr David Arnold, Chief Accountant **4**_____
D.L. Cromer Ltd. **5**_____ Staines, Middlesex. He advised us
to contact you as a referee concerning the credit
facilities which his company has asked us **6**_____.

Could you confirm that the company settles **7**_____ due
dates, and is sound enough to meet credits of from £3,000
8_____ £5,000?

We would be most grateful **9**_____ a reply **10**_____ your
earliest convenience.

Yours sincerely,

Patricia Gómez (Sra.)

Sales Manager

4 Reply to request for a reference

Mr MacFee has made some brief notes before writing a reply to Sra. Gómez's letter (see Exercise 3). As Mr MacFee, write the letter. Include the sender's and inside addresses, and an appropriate date.

> replying yr. letter 18 May re. D.L. Cromer Ltd.
> excellent reputation in UK - customer of ours for a long time
> credit limit w. us a little lower than the one you mentioned, but
> always settle on or before due dates
> grateful if treat this info. in strictest confidence

5 Unfavourable reply

When replying to enquiries about credit rating, it is better not to mention the company's name or to be too specific in the details you give. Rewrite the letter below considering this advice.

Dear Ms Allard

I am replying to your enquiry of 19 September about Fit-a-Part Ltd.

We have allowed Fit-a-Part credit in the past three years, but only up to £2,000, not the £10,000 you mentioned. We have also found that they need four or five reminders before clearing their account.

Please treat this information in the strictest confidence.

Yours sincerely

P.M. Lord

Accountant

6 Words and definitions

Make words from the jumbled letters and match them with the definitions below.

a DAB TEDB
b TDREIC TAINRG
c LIBL FO CAXNEGEH
d TLAFEDU
e ERECEENRF
f DERCTI STILFCIIAE

1 Means of allowing credit, e.g. bill of exchange.
2 Debt that is not likely to be paid.
3 Method of payment by which the seller can give the buyer credit for an agreed period, e.g. 30 days.
4 Evaluation of the creditworthiness of an individual or company.
5 To fail to do something required by law.
6 Written report on a company's creditworthiness.

9
Banking

1 Reporting verbs

Read the sentences below. Then find the reporting verb from the box which best fits each situation. The first one has been done for you.

| explain | promise | thank | admit |
| suggest | advise | refuse | apologize |

1 I am grateful to you for sending the shipping documents so promptly.
   thank

2 Why don't you think it over for a few days and then get back to me?
   _____

3 Unfortunately, we cannot extend your overdraft.
   _____

4 I think you should consider our terms before making a decision.
   _____

5 I'll definitely let you have the details tomorrow.
   _____

6 It appears that we made an error on your October statement.
   _____

7 We understand that the bank will want about 120% in securities to cover this credit.
   _____

8 I am sorry for the delay in replying to you.
   _____

2 Word forms

Complete the sentences below, using the correct form of the words in brackets. The first one has been done for you.

1 Lack of capital will *endanger* the project. (*danger*)
2 The exporter opens a letter of credit by _____ an application form. (*complete*)
3 The cheque should be made _____ to International Boats Ltd. (*pay*)
4 The shipping documents include bill of lading, _____ certificate, and invoice. (*insure*)
5 I am pleased to inform you that your _____ has now been extended to £4,000. (*overdraw*)
6 Loans can be extended only by _____ with the Branch Manager. (*arrange*)

7 You will receive _____ of payment from our bank. (*confirm*)

8 Your _____ should appear twice on the document. (*sign*)

9 We need a loan to secure the _____ of our company. (*expand*)

10 With _____ to our telephone conversation yesterday, I am writing to confirm our agreement. (*refer*)

3 Bill of exchange

Complete the bill of exchange below with the following information:

- Payment is due 60 days after date.
- There is only one bill, therefore write *sola*. For this reason, there is no need to write anything before the words *to the order of* as there is only one bill (otherwise this line would have *second of the same tenor and date unpaid* to show there was a second copy).
- The bill is for $28,000.
- It was drawn on 28 February 20—.
- The drawer is Hartley–Mason Inc.
- In (6), write in the words of the currency that is being used and the actual words of the amount.
- In *Value Received* write *payable at the current rate of exchange for bankers' drafts in London.*
- The bill is being drawn on Glough & Book Motorcycles Ltd, 31–37 Trades Street, Nottingham, NG1 3AA.
- The drawer's name is Hartley-Mason Inc., 618 West and Vine Street, Chicago, Illinois, and will be signed by Mr J.R. Mason, the President of the Company.

At **1**_____ pay this **2**_____ Bill of Exchange

2_____ to the order of Number 4003 1 3021

Exchange for **3**_____ **4**_____

5_____

6_____

Value Received **7**_____

placed to account

To

8_____

_____

_____

_____

For and on behalf of

9_____

_____

_____

_____

Signed

9_____

_____

4 Request for a loan

Read the following conversation between a bank manager, John Steele, and a customer, Richard Grey.

JOHN STEELE Good afternoon, Mr Grey. Now, how can I help you?

RICHARD GREY Well, I know my company's been going through a bad time recently, but I would like to expand the fleet by buying another two trucks. I wonder if you could extend my loan to cover the investment?

JOHN STEELE I'm afraid we can't extend your existing loan, but we may be able to offer a bridging loan. How much would you need?

RICHARD GREY Probably around £50,000, I think, to buy two second-hand vehicles. I'm sure that the revenue from the extra trucks would allow me to repay you within a year.

JOHN STEELE What can you offer as security for the loan?

RICHARD GREY Just the trucks themselves.

JOHN STEELE Well, unfortunately, I am not in a position to make an independent decision – I shall have to consult our directors – but I promise I will consult them this week, and let you know as soon as possible.

RICHARD GREY Thank you very much.

As John Steele, summarize the conversation in a memo to the bank's Board of Directors. Try to use some of the reporting verbs from Exercise 1. Remember only to report the details which will help the Board to make a decision. Head the memo 'Strictly confidential', and start like this:

I had a meeting with Mr Richard Grey, of RG Logistics Ltd, on 17 September…

5 Refusing a loan

The bank's Board of Directors has now discussed Mr Grey's request for a loan (see Exercise 4). This is their reply to his memo.

Memo

From:	Secretary to the Directors
To:	John Steele
Subject:	Bridging loan, RG Logistics Ltd
Date:	21 September 20—

STRICTLY CONFIDENTIAL

With reference to your memo dated 19 September concerning the above loan, the Board regret that in this case they are unable to offer Mr Grey the credit requested. They would be grateful if you could inform Mr Grey that it is the bank's policy only to offer substantial loans against negotiable securities such as shares or bonds.

As John Steele write a letter to Mr Grey, explaining that credit has been refused. Suggest that there are other sources he could try, for example a finance corporation, but warn him that their interest rates are likely to be significantly higher than the bank's.

6 Words and definitions

Make words from the jumbled letters and match them with the definitions below.

a SRDNEOE
b TCENRAUOMYD CIERTD
c FIRCETETACI FO IGIRNO
d EALNC LBLI
e SYAD TFARE HSITG
f CHAREMNT NBKA
g AREODVHE
h TGISH TFRDA

1 Transfer a bill or cheque by signing it on the back.
2 Type of bank that specializes in international trade and finance.
3 Document that shows where goods were made.
4 Bill of exchange without any accompanying documents.
5 Letter of credit that requires the seller to supply shipping documents to a bank to obtain payment.
6 Number of days within which a bill of exchange must be paid after presentation.
7 Regular cost of running a company, e.g. rent.
8 Bill of exchange that must be paid immediately it is presented.

7 Abbreviations

Complete the full term for each abbreviation.
The first one has been done for you.

1 B/E   B __ __ l O __   E __ cha __ g __
2 D/P   __ __ c __ __ e n __ __   A __ a __ n s __
      __ __ y __ __ __ t
3 L/C   __ __ tt __ __   O __   __ r __ d __ __ __
4 D/A   __ o __ um __ __ __ __ s   __ ga __ __ st
      __ c __ ep __ a __ __ e
5 E&OE __ rr __ __ s   an __
      __ mi __ __ __ __ on __   __ xc __ p __ __ d
6 DC   __ o __ um __ __ t __ __ y   __ __ e __ __ t
7 CP   __ ar __ __ ag __   __ ai __
8 D/S   __ __ y __   Af __ __ r   __ __ gh __
9 IMO   __ nt __ __ __ at __ __ __ __ l
      __ __ n __ y   __ r __ er
10 CF   __ __ rr __ a __ e   __ or __ a __ __

8 Documentary credit 1

Letter from the confirming bank to the exporters

Paul Diderot, Documentary Credits Manager of the Banque de Lyon, writes to exporters Château Wines, informing them that a letter of credit has been opened for them. Choose the correct expressions from the box to fill the gaps.

inform	charges	documents	draw	acting	valid	settle	opened

BANQUE DE LYON

500 boulevard Jobert
69000 Lyon
Tél: +33 4 781243
Fax: +33 4 781244
Email: pdiderot@banque-lyon.co.fr

8 July 20—

Mr James Freeland
Château Wines
80 rue Gaspart-André
69003 Lyon

Dear Mr Freeland

L/C No. 340895/AGL

We are **1**_____ on behalf of the Eastland Bank, London, and would like to **2**_____ you that the above documentary credit for €5,300 has been **3**_____ in your favour by your customers BestValue Ltd. The credit is **4**_____ until 12 August and all bank **5**_____ have been paid.

Please send the following **6**_____ to the above address:

- Air waybill
- Invoice for full value of the sale CIF London
- Insurance certificate

Would you also **7**_____ a sight draft for the full amount of the invoice on us so that we can **8**_____ this account.

Thank you in advance.

Yours faithfully

Paul Diderot

Manager, Documentary Credits

9 Documentary credit 2

Letter from the exporters to the confirming bank

James Freeland of Château Wines has made some notes for his reply to Paul Diderot's letter. Write out the letter in full.

> thank for advice of 8 Jly. shipment to BestValue in UK now effected.
>
> encl. shipping documents you request + draft for € 5,300.00.
>
> pl. accept draft and remit proceeds to our account Banque de Commerce,
>
> 28 rue Gaspart-André, 69002, Lyon. NB list documents

10
Agents and agencies

1 Find the keyword

Complete the boxes with the missing word from the sentences below to find the keyword down.

ACROSS

1 Shares are bought and sold on a _____ _____ . (2 words: 5,8)
2 _____ houses receive orders from overseas, place them, and make arrangements for packing, shipping, and insurance.
3 A _____ _____ is the only one allowed to sell the products of a manufacturer in a particular area. (2 words: 4,5)
4 An agent who sells products on a _____ basis makes a certain amount of money for each item sold.
5 A _____ is a person or organization that hires an agent to buy or sell goods for them.
6 In non-recourse _____ , a firm buys up outstanding invoices and claims the debts.
7 _____ invoice value is the value of an invoice without extra charges.
8 _____ markets are where items like coffee, cocoa, and rubber are bought and sold.
9 Agents who take the risk of being liable for customers' debts may receive a _____ _____ commission. (2 words: 3,7)
10 A _____ _____ is an organization that buys goods on behalf of a principal. (2 words: 6,5)
11 A prospective agent may need to be convinced that there is a _____ for the principal's products.

DOWN

12 Keyword: The basis on which an agent is employed to resell goods for a commission.

2 Phrasal verbs

Using a word from column A and a word from column B, complete each sentence with a phrasal verb. The first one has been done for you.

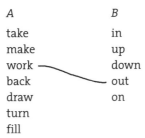

A	B
take	in
make	up
work	down
back	out
draw	on
turn	
fill	

1 I am sure it will be possible for us to _work_ _out_ a more satisfactory arrangement for promoting your products.

2 We would be pleased to _____ _____ an initial one-year contract to act as your sole agents.

3 We will _____ _____ a draft agreement and send it to you as soon as possible.

4 We plan to _____ _____ the advertising campaign with supplies of brochures and leaflets to all our dealers.

5 I regret that we must _____ _____ your offer of a sole agency because at present we do not have sufficient resources.

6 Please will you _____ _____ the cheque to Wallis Greene Ltd, our distributors in your area.

7 It will be necessary to _____ _____ the enclosed customs form.

8 As we have been trading for over a year, it will not be necessary for us to _____ _____ references.

3 Offer of an agency

Choose the best words from the options in brackets in this letter offering an agency.

Grazioli S.p.A.

Via Gradenigo 134
50133 Firenze

☎ +39 (0)55 89-65-20
🖨 +39 (0)55 89-65-21
🖥 pgrazioli@grazioli.co.it

Herr Otto Grassmann
Grassmann AG
Lindenweg 18
D–1000 Berlin 12

23 October 20—

Dear Herr Grassmann

You were recommended to us by the German Chamber of Commerce, who
1_____ (*said, told, spoke*) you might be interested in representing
a leading Italian glass manufacturer in your country.

We have a number of agencies in other European countries who receive products
on **2**_____ (*commission, consignment, approval*), then sell them on a
6% commission on ex-works prices. These are **3**_____ (*single, unique, sole*)
agencies.

Generally, their customers **4**_____ (*settle, agree, deal*) all accounts with us,
then we supply them direct on invoices received from the agent.

In most cases we offer a **5**_____ (*test, proof, trial*) agency for one year, and if
the results are good, we **6**_____ (*export, extend, expand*) the agency
agreement on a further two-year contract. We would **7**_____ (*offer, suggest,
invite*) you support through advertising, brochures, and leaflets in German, the
8_____ (*cost, value, worth*) of this being shared between us.

Our market **9**_____ (*researchers, reporters, informers*) tell us there is an
increasing demand for our line of products in your country, so it would not be difficult to
sell our products.

If you would be interested in an agency of this type, we can send you a standard
agreement, giving you more details of our terms. Meanwhile, we are enclosing our
10_____ (*actual, present, current*) catalogue.

Yours sincerely

Pietro Grazioli

Chairman

Encl.

4 Reply to an offer of an agency

Choose the phrase or sentence from each group which would be most appropriate in a reply to the letter in Exercise 3. Write out the reply as a letter. Include the inside address, date, salutation, complimentary close, and signature block, and divide it into paragraphs.

1 a Thanks very much for your letter the other day.
  b I was delighted when I received your recent communication.
  c Thank you for your letter of 23 October.

2 a I can confirm that we would be interested in representing you, but not on a sole agency basis, as this would restrict our sales.
  b We might be interested in representing you, but we can't go ahead on a sole agency basis as we've got to sell a lot.
  c Were it not for the sole agency basis you mention, your proposal might be received more favourably.

3 a Not only that, but we want a cut of 10% and three quarters of the ads paid by you.
  b In addition, a 10% commission on ex-works prices and 75% support in advertising are the basis on which we might contemplate negotiating an agreement.
  c Also, our usual terms are a 10% commission on ex-works prices and 75% of the advertising costs.

4 a Notwithstanding, we were overwhelmed by the superlative quality of the products in your catalogue.
  b In spite of our objections about terms, the products in your catalogue look really good.
  c However, we were very impressed by the high quality of the products in your catalogue.

5 a If you are able to revise your terms, we would be interested in receiving a draft contract.
  b Subject to a satisfactory revision of terms, a draft contract would be worthy of our consideration.
  c If you can look at your terms again, send us a contract.

6 a Give us a call sometime, so we can have a chat.
  b I look forward to hearing from you.
  c I remain your humble servant.

5 Request for an agency

Read this request to act as a buying agent from Manfred Kobelt, Managing Director of the Kobelt Agency. Choose the correct words from the box to fill the gaps.

offer	commission	principals
rates	documentation	freight
del credere	recommendation	terms
factory	manufacturers	brochure

The Kobelt Agency

Brauneggerstr. 618
D–4400 Münster
Tel: +49 251 37–25–94
Fax: +49 251 37–25–95
Email: kobeltm@kobeltagency.co.de

24 June 20—

Mrs Cristina Neves
Buying Manager
Portuguese Industrial Importers
Rua dos Santos 179
1200 Lisbon
Portugal

Dear Mrs Neves

We are writing to you on the **1**_____ of the Portuguese Chamber of Commerce, who informed us that you were looking for a buying agent for precision tools in this country.

We have been in this trade for over twenty years and have close contacts with the major **2**_____ both here and overseas.

We would like to give you a brief outline of the **3**_____ we work on. Generally, we place orders for our **4**_____ with our suppliers, and our customers settle direct with the manufacturer. In addition, we arrange all costs, insurance, and **5**_____ facilities for the client, handling consignments from the **6**_____ to the port / airport of the importer's country.

As we have dealt with these agencies for a number of years, we can offer you their most competitive **7**_____ for shipment. In addition, we would take care of all **8**_____ , including customs formalities.

As a rule we operate on a 4.5% **9**_____ on CIF values, but if credit is involved, we could offer **10**_____ services for an additional 2.5% commission, pending the usual inquiries.

If you are interested in this **11**_____ we can assure you of first class, efficient service. Please contact us if you need any more information. I have enclosed our **12**_____ giving you full details of our company.

We look forward to hearing from you in due course.
Yours sincerely

Manfred Kobelt

Manfred Kobelt
Managing Director

Enc.

6 Reply to a request for an agency

Cristina Neves has decided to email her reply to Herr Kobelt's letter (see Exercise 5). Draft an email from the notes below. Remember that she does not know him so the style will be quite formal, like a letter.

> *Kobelt*
> – *Thank for letter – interested in proposals – increasing demand for precision tools here*
> – *In principle, cld. accept either 3% comm. on CIF values or the 2.5% del credere comm.*
> – *Can Kobelt act as clearing and forwarding agency, offering door-to-door facility?*
> – *Kobelt willing to send contact details of 2 companies they act for who can offer references? If yes, we wld. be interested in discussing contract*
> – *Look forward to hearing, etc.*

11
Transportation and shipping

1 Two-word terms

Match words from box A with words from box B to make two-word terms used in business correspondence. Then use the terms to complete the sentences below.

A	
shipping	bulk
charter	delivery
air	all
forwarding	shipping

B	
risks	waybill
note	party
agent	note
mark	carrier

1 Packing and shipment will be arranged by our ____ ____ .
2 The freighter *Narvik* is a ____ ____ with a cargo capacity of six thousand tons.
3 When you have confirmed the charter, we will send you the ____ ____ for signature.
4 Before signing the ____ ____ , please check that the consignment has arrived undamaged.
5 The cost of freight London Heathrow – Dubai is £10.00 per kilo, plus £8.00 ____ ____ , and £60.00 customs clearance and handling.
6 Please would you arrange insurance cover for £100,000 against ____ ____ .
7 Enclosed you will find our standard ____ ____ and bill of lading.
8 The ____ ____ on the sides of the crates should correspond with the one on your shipping documents.

2 Formal and informal English

Rewrite these sentences in a more polite form, using the words supplied. The first one has been done for you.

1 Fill in the despatch form and don't forget to let us have it with the parcels. (*please, send, consignment*)
Please fill in the despatch form and send it to us with the consignment.

2 If you don't understand, get in touch with me. (*queries, hesitate, contact*)
_____
_____

3 I've had a word with Despatch, who say there was nothing wrong with the crockery when they sent it off. (*checked, Department, records, perfect condition*)
_____
_____

4 We want a quote for picking up ten armchairs here and taking them to R. Hughes & Son Ltd, Swansea.
(*please, collection, consignment, above address, delivery*)

_____

_____

5 The loss on invoice value must be £300.00 and we want our money back.
(*estimate, claiming compensation, amount*)

_____

_____

6 Do you want us to send the goods back to you, or to keep them here for you to look at? (*prefer, return, hold, inspection*)

_____

_____

3 Enquiry to a forwarding agent

Complete this fax enquiring about a forwarding agent's charges with the correct prepositions.

Fax

York Instrumentation Ltd
157 Links Road, Derby
DE7 8PX
Tel: +44 (0)1332 491567
Fax: +44 (0)1332 491568

To: Bill Crowley, Landmark Freight Services
From: Stephen Lang
Subject: Quotation
Fax no.: 796543
Page(s): 2 (incl. this page)
Date: 10 November 20—

Dear Mr Crowley

You were recommended **1**_____ us **2**_____ Stellman Ltd, our

associates, **3**_____ whom you have operated as forwarding agents.

We are looking **4**_____ a reliable agent to handle our deliveries

5_____ Europe, taking care **6**_____ documentation and making sure

7_____ safe delivery – many **8**_____ our products are very fragile.

You will find a list representing a consignment we wish to send

9_____ Lausanne **10**_____ road. Could you let us have your quotation,

and if it is competitive, we can assure you **11**_____ further business

12_____ the future.

Yours sincerely

STEPHEN LANG

York Instrumentation Ltd

4 Forwarding agent's reply

Below is Bill Crowley's reply to Stephen Lang (see Exercise 3). Write it out, putting the phrases in the correct order and adding paragraphs, capitals, and punctuation where necessary.

Fax

Landmark Freight Services Ltd
Unit 7B, Barrow Business Park,
Derby
DE12 8ER
Tel.: +44 (0)1332 796537
Fax: +44 (0)1332 796543

To: S. Lang, York Instrumentation
From: Bill Crowley
Fax no.:   491568
Subject: Quotation
Date: 11 November 20—
Page/s: 2

Dear Mr Lang

— our freight charges / of 10 November / thank you / enquiring about / for your fax
— for shipments / I enclose / which includes all transport customs and documentation charges / our tariff list
— are highly competitive / I think / that these rates / you will find
— that we have / in handling fragile consignments / in addition / extensive experience / I can confirm
— and I will be very pleased / any further questions / please contact me / to help / if you have
— to hearing / I look forward / from you

Yours sincerely

Bill Crowley

5 Words and definitions

Make words from the jumbled letters and match them with the definitions below.

a LPDOAYA
b NDSEERO
c LSDCAUE
d ODTMLMILAU

e EIRTCEP
f NOSTDINOCALOI
g PIBKRORSHE
h RECNOTNIA

1 When small consignments from different exporters are loaded into a single container.
2 Document showing that goods have been paid for.
3 Unit of transportation, e.g. a container, that can be transferred between different systems, e.g. train and ship.
4 Agent who arranges the transport of cargo by ship.
5 The part of a cargo that earns money for the shipping company.
6 Large metal box in which goods are packed for transportation.
7 Term used on a bill of lading to indicate that goods were damaged or incomplete when they came on board.
8 To transfer a cheque or bill of exchange to someone else by signing it on the back.

6 Enquiry to a container company

John Merton, Sales Manager of Glaston Potteries, emails his PA, Jill Bradley, asking her to send an email to National Containers. As Jill Bradley, draft the email. Start: *I am contacting you on behalf of John Merton concerning…*

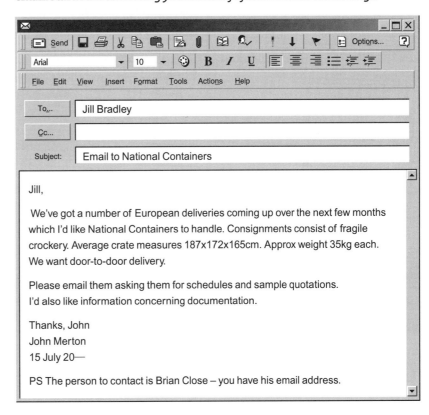

To… Jill Bradley

Cc…

Subject: Email to National Containers

Jill,

We've got a number of European deliveries coming up over the next few months which I'd like National Containers to handle. Consignments consist of fragile crockery. Average crate measures 187x172x165cm. Approx weight 35kg each. We want door-to-door delivery.

Please email them asking them for schedules and sample quotations.
I'd also like information concerning documentation.

Thanks, John
John Merton
15 July 20—

PS The person to contact is Brian Close – you have his email address.

7 Container company's reply   This is Brian Close's reply to Jill Bradley (see Exercise 6). He has written the
email but not yet checked it through. Find and correct the mistakes – there are
ten of them.

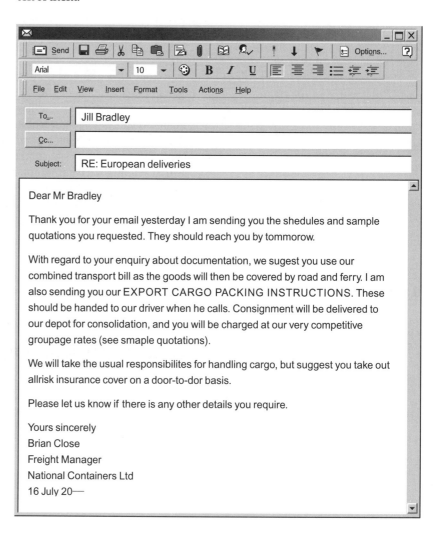

12
Insurance

1 Terms used in insurance

Complete the missing terms used in insurance. Each blank stands for a missing letter.

1 An i _ _ _ _ _ _ _ _ company indemnifies clients against loss.

2 Underwriters at Lloyds work in groups called
s _ _ _ _ _ _ _ _.

3 An insurance p _ _ _ _ _ is a contract taken out to protect someone against future risks.

4 Clients are i _ _ _ _ _ _ _ _ _ against loss or damage when they have insurance policies.

5 A p _ _ _ _ _ is the amount of money paid to an insurance company for cover.

6 L _ _ _ _ ' _ List is a daily newspaper about shipping movements and cargo markets.

7 A p _ _ _ _ _ _ form is completed by a firm or person who wants insurance cover.

8 A client sends their insurance company a c _ _ _ _ form when they have suffered damage or loss.

9 Under f _ _ _ _ _ _ bonds, companies can insure themselves against dishonest employees.

10 The job of an average a _ _ _ _ _ _ _ is to examine damage and estimate compensation.

2 Request for comprehensive insurance

Read the following request for comprehensive insurance and choose the best words from the options in brackets.

HUMBOLDT EXPORTERS LTD

Exode House | 115 Tremona Road | Southampton SO9 4XY

Telephone: +44 (0)23 80 149783
Fax: +44 (0)23 80 149784
Email: hindp@humboldt.co.uk

15 February 20—

International Insurance plc
153 Western Road
Brighton
Sussex
BN1 4EX

Dear Sir

We are a **1**_____ (*grand, large, wide*) export company
2_____ (*who, which, what*) ships consignments
3_____ (*in, to, towards*) Europe and North America. We
4_____ (*want, would like, request*) to know if you can
5_____ (*suggest, supply, present*) us with a quotation for a
comprehensive policy, **6**_____ (*assuring, protecting, covering*)
our warehouse at Dock Road, Southampton.

We would like the policy to **7**_____ (*consist, contain, include*)
fire, flood, theft, burglary, and the usual contingencies
affecting this **8**_____ (*form, kind, variety*) of enterprise.
At any one time, there may be about £800,000 in stock on the
9_____ (*premises, grounds, floors*).

If you can give us a **10**_____ (*competing, competition,
competitive*) quote, we will **11**_____ (*think, imagine, consider*)
taking out further policies with you.

We look forward to hearing from you **12**_____ (*soon, presently,
immediately*).

Yours faithfully

Peter Hind

Company Secretary

3 Reply to request for comprehensive insurance

Below is an email from Gerald Croft, Regional Manager of International Insurance, to Natalie Weston, his secretary, asking her to draft a reply to Peter Hind's letter (see Exercise 2). As Natalie Weston, draft the reply for Gerald Croft to sign.

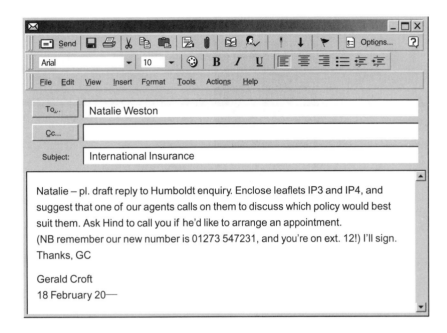

To... Natalie Weston

Cc...

Subject: International Insurance

Natalie – pl. draft reply to Humboldt enquiry. Enclose leaflets IP3 and IP4, and suggest that one of our agents calls on them to discuss which policy would best suit them. Ask Hind to call you if he'd like to arrange an appointment.
(NB remember our new number is 01273 547231, and you're on ext. 12!) I'll sign.
Thanks, GC

Gerald Croft
18 February 20—

4 Claim for fire damage

Humboldt Exporters insured their Southampton Warehouse with International Insurance (see Exercises 2 and 3), but unfortunately suffered a fire a few months later. Mr Hind has made some notes for an email telling International Insurance about the fire and asking them to send a claim form. Write the email.

policy no. 439178/D
regret fire broke out in S'ton warehouse early y'day. extensive damage (approx. £7,000) to textiles stored for shipment. fire service has provided evidence that electrical fault was cause. pl. send claim form asap.

5 **Request for open cover**

There are no capitals, punctuation, or paragraphs in this letter requesting open cover. Write out the letter correctly. Divide the body of the letter into four paragraphs.

Brunel House
Brunel Street
Liverpool L2 2ER

☎ +44 (0)151 630876
📠 +44 (0)151 630877
💻 jturner@ukengineering.co.uk

1 may 20—

sugden & able
insurance brokers
63 grover street
manchester m5 6ld

dear sir madam

we are a large engineering company exporting machine parts worldwide and have a contract to supply a middle eastern customer for the next two years as the parts we will be supplying are similar in nature and are going to the same destination over this period we would prefer to insure them under an open cover policy would you be willing to provide open cover for £500,000 against all risks for this period i look forward to hearing from you yours faithfully

jack turner

shipping manager

6 Reply to request for open cover

Alan Able, Director of Sugden and Able, asks his secretary, Mary Todd, to reply to Jack Turner's letter (see Exercise 5). Read their conversation and, as Mary Todd, write the email. (Alan Able's telephone number is 0161 542783.)

ALAN ABLE Oh, and Mary, could you email UK Engineering – Jack Turner I think the chap's name was – anyway, the email's on the letterhead. Thank him for his enquiry and tell him that we offer two types of cover, either of which might suit them.

MARY TODD Which ones do you mean?

ALAN ABLE The floating policy – that would cover all the shipments they plan to make up to an agreed maximum value, and can be renewed when necessary.

MARY TODD And the other one?

ALAN ABLE Open cover – that's the one he seems to know something about, but you'd better explain it anyway. It's where we provide cover for all shipments over a given period. Tell him I'd be very pleased to discuss these options if he'd like to give me a call.

13
Miscellaneous correspondence

1 Prepositions

Make eight complete sentences used in general and social correspondence by joining phrases from column A and phrases from column B with one of the prepositions. You will need to use some of the prepositions more than once, but each phrase should be used only once. The first sentence has been done for you.

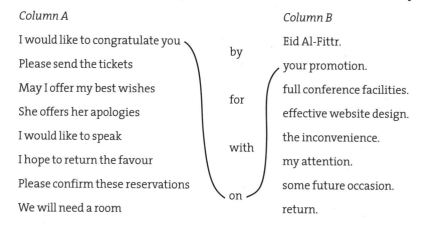

Column A

I would like to congratulate you

Please send the tickets

May I offer my best wishes

She offers her apologies

I would like to speak

I hope to return the favour

Please confirm these reservations

We will need a room

by

for

with

on

Column B

Eid Al-Fittr.

your promotion.

full conference facilities.

effective website design.

the inconvenience.

my attention.

some future occasion.

return.

2 Formal and informal English

Complete the following sentences so that they have a similar meaning to the one above, but are more suitable for formal business correspondence.

1 He's sorry he can't come, but hopes he can come another time.
   He sends his _____ .

2 It's such a shame that your brother is ill. I'm really sorry.
   I was sorry _____ .

3 So you've been elected Chairman of the company! Well done!
   I would like _____ .

4 Mr Norman wants to drop in on you next week about the contract.
   Mr Norman would _____ .

5 Mr Chung can't see you on Friday for your appointment after all.
   Unfortunately, _____ .

6 Can you come to our Sales Conference on 18 March?
   We would like _____ .

7 Thanks for helping me while I was in Hamburg last week.
   I would _____ .

8 It'll be good to see you on Friday.
   I look _____ .

3 Conference facilities

Diane Taylor, Sales Director of Data Unlimited plc, has emailed her PA, Lynn Paul, with details of a sales conference she is planning for December. As Lynn Paul, draft the letter she mentions.

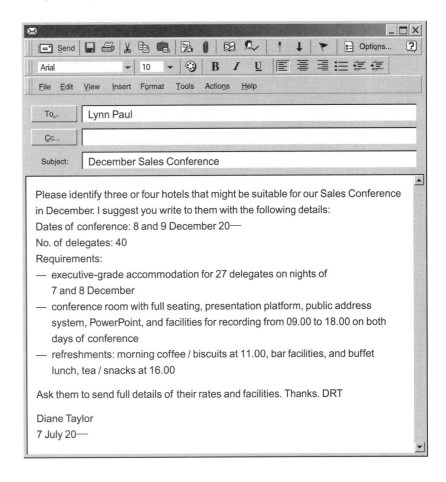

4 Hotel reservation

Diane Taylor chose the Royal Hotel for Data Unlimited's sales conference (see Exercise 3). It is now only a few days before the conference and two delegates, Charles Bickford and Claire Ramal, have made a last-minute decision to stay at the hotel. As Lynn Paul, complete the fax below. Ask the hotel if they have two extra rooms available and apologize for the short notice.

Fax

Data Unlimited plc
Data House
Chertsey Road
Twickenham
TW1 1EP
Telephone: +44 (0)20 81 460259
Fax: +44 (0)20 81 985132

To: _____
From: _____
Fax: 01372 908754
Subject: _____
Date: 3 December
Page/s: 1

5 Invitation

Read this invitation from a Chamber of Commerce and choose the best words from the options in brackets.

Dear Herr Boldt

We **1**_____ (*wish, want, would like*) to invite
you to our annual dinner on 15 February, and
2_____ (*wonder, ask, demand*) if you would consider being
one of our guest **3**_____ (*announcers, speakers, talkers*).

Our theme this year is 'The effects of the euro', and
we would **4**_____ (*admire, seek, appreciate*) a
contribution from your field of manufacturing on how this is
5_____ (*afflicting, affecting, altering*) you and your
colleagues enterprises. Please **6**_____ (*let, leave, make*)
us know as soon as possible if you are able to
7_____ (*talk, speak, discuss*).

8_____ (*Inside, Enclosed, Within*) you will find a formal
invitation for yourself and a guest.

Yours sincerely

Peter House

Chairman

6 Accepting an invitation

Below is Herr Boldt's reply to Peter House (see Exercise 5). Write it out, putting the phrases in the correct order and adding paragraphs, capitals, and punctuation where necessary.

Dear Mr House

for your letter / inviting me to speak / on 15 February /
thank you / at your annual dinner

I am honoured / your kind invitation / to accept

I would like to focus / on the cost of raw materials /
in my talk / on the effects that the euro is having

and would welcome / you care to make / I will send you /
next week / any comments or suggestions / a transcript

to meeting you / very much / I look forward /
on February 15

Yours sincerely

Gunther Boldt

Chairman

14
Memos and reports

1 Formal and informal English

Match the sentences in column A with sentences in column B with similar meanings. Then put a tick by the sentences which are more suitable for a formal memo.

Column A

1 We haven't decided so far.

2 No-one will lose their job because of what we're doing.

3 Your cooperation in this matter is essential.

4 He's always off sick so he's leaving.

5 The company has expanded a lot recently.

6 Please see your manager if you have any questions.

7 Staff should close windows and take personal belongings with them.

8 The staff restaurant will be relocated in the near future.

Column B

a The last few months have seen a period of unprecedented growth.

b Have a word with your boss if you don't understand.

c No firm decision has yet been reached.

d Don't forget to take your coat and bag, and shut the windows.

e You've got to do what we say.

f We're going to move the canteen.

g There will be no redundancies as a result of this measure.

h He has decided to retire on the grounds of ill-health.

2 Memo about documentary credits

The Finance Director of your company, Interbank, has asked you to write a memo reminding staff how important it is to carefully check all details of documents associated with documentary credits. £250,000 has been lost in the past year over mistakes in effecting documentary credit transactions. Select the five most relevant points from the check list below and, as his PA, write the memo.

- Check that all trains are running on time.
- Check all transport documents, insurance certificates, invoices and customs clearance certificates.
- Check staff holidays have been arranged for this year.
- Check details of hotels in the local areas.
- Check bills of exchange and letters of credit.
- Check the spelling in the names of the parties is correct.
- Check if local events will interfere with our hotel bookings.
- Check that places of departure and destinations are correct.
- Check the right amounts for the transactions are listed and the correct currencies have been written in.
- Check salary scales for the members of the Documentary Credit Department.

3 Memo about fraud

Terry Fairman is the Chief Accountant at National Stores plc. He has just attended a Directors' meeting about fraud when customers pay by cheque, and has been asked to write a memo to sales staff about this problem. As Terry Fairman, write the memo, selecting information from the notes he made at the meeting. It should cover the following points:
- what the problem is
- what practical measures sales staff should take to reduce it

---

1 Sales staff should carefully match signatures on cheque cards with those on cheques.

2 The value of bad cheques presented over the past year amounts to over £50,000.

3 Sales staff should not make customers feel like criminals.

4 Most customers use a credit card or cash to pay for goods.

5 Write the cheque card number and expiry date on the back of the cheque.

6 Supervisors should be contacted if sales staff are unsure about a payment.

7 Customers' reactions should be noted for nervousness.

8 Cheques should be examined to see that they have been completed properly.

9 Banks also lose a great deal of money through cheque fraud.

10 The problem of bad cheques cannot be eliminated, but sales staff can help reduce it significantly.

---

4 Reports: past tenses

Complete the following extracts from reports, using either the present perfect continuous (e.g. *have been working*) or the simple past (e.g. *worked*).

EXTRACT 1

Our organization **1**_____ (*export*) precision tools to the Middle East for over forty years. We **2**_____ (*open*) our first office in Iraq in the early 1960s and it **3**_____ (*remain*) open for five years until we **4**_____ (*move*) our headquarters to Jordan. In the last few months we **5**_____ (*negotiate*) a contract with Saudi Arabia, which we hope will be signed soon.

EXTRACT 2

Since the beginning of this year, the department store **6**_____ (*lose*) over £5,000 per month due to theft, and last month this **7**_____ (*rise*) to £8,500. We believe that a gang of shoplifters **8**_____ (*operate*) in the building for the last few weeks, and that this may account for the losses that **9**_____ (*occur*) in June. Over the last few days we **10**_____ (*have*) discussions with our security consultants who will produce a report shortly.

EXTRACT 3

Trading in the market **11**_____ (*be*) slack for the first two months of the year, as investors **12**_____ (*feel*) worried by the uncertain political climate, and interest rates **13**_____ (*remain*) high. However, in the last few weeks, interest rates **14**_____ (*fall*) gradually and look as if they will continue to do so. Investors **15**_____ (*return*) to the market slowly and volumes **16**_____ (increase).

5 Report on introduction of flexitime

John Holland, Company Secretary of Elland Hughes Advertising, has been asked to prepare a report on the introduction of a flexitime system. Read Documents 1, 2, 3, and 4 carefully. Then, as John Holland, write the report. It should take the following form:

- Introduction: give details of the proposed flexitime system.
- Outline the advantages of the system to the company.
- Outline the advantages of the system to the staff.
- Mention the financial costs and benefits.
- Make your conclusions and recommendations.

DOCUMENT 1
Memo from the Chief Executive

Memo

To: John Holland
From: Ian Peters
Date: 12 February 20——
Subject: Flexitime

The Board have recently been considering the introduction of a flexitime system. Please prepare a report on the feasibility of introducing this system. The report should cover:

- Staff attitude towards flexitime
- Benefits to the company of flexitime
- Financial implications
- Disadvantages (if any)
- Conclusions and recommendations

We propose that the new times might be from 07.00 to 21.00. Staff would be able to choose their hours of work between these times, and could have a weekday off in lieu of Saturday if they prefer.

Please let me have the report and your findings by 18 March.

Results of staff questionnaire

1 Are you in favour of the introduction of a flexitime system?

Yes	87%
No	4%
Don't know	9%

2 Would you prefer to have a day off in the week instead of Saturday?

Yes	76%
No	11%
Don't know	13%

3 Which facilities do you find most crowded?

Photocopiers	35%
Fax machines	24%
Canteen	21%
Toilet	3%
Other	2%

4 What is your average journey time to work during the rush hour?

Less than ½ hour	12%
½ hour to 1 hour	29%
1 hour to 1½ hours	48%
More than 1½ hours	11%

5 If flexitime were introduced, which hours would you prefer?

7 a.m. to 3 p.m.	18%
8 a.m. to 4 p.m.	21%
9 a.m. to 5 p.m.	16%
10 a.m. to 6 p.m.	20%
11 a.m. to 7 p.m.	10%
midday to 8 p.m.	10%
1 p.m. to 9 p.m.	5%

6 If the office was open six days a week, which day would you choose to have free in addition to Sunday?

Monday	16%
Tuesday	7%
Wednesday	23%
Thursday	14%
Friday	19%
Saturday	21%

7 What would be the main advantage of a free day during the week for you?

Being with partner	34%
Shopping	23%
Making other appointments	17%

8 In what way would the company benefit most from a flexitime system?

Clients in different time zones would find it easier to contact us	34%
Clients could contact us on Saturday	26%
Staff would not be tired after the rush-hour	24%
Security would be improved	12%
Other	4%

9 Would you be in favour of the introduction of a clocking-in system?

Yes	26%
No	48%
Don't know	26%

10 Would you be in favour of a one-year trial period?

Yes	76%
No	14%
Don't know	10%

DOCUMENT 3
Selection of comments from '*Do you have any other comments?*' section on staff questionnaire

'A great idea – I'm sure we'd all work better.'

'I'd be able to spend more time with my family.'

'Would make all the difference if I didn't have to get to work in the rush hour.'

'Could take the kids to school, which would help a lot.'

DOCUMENT 4
Memo from the Accounts Department

Memo

To: John Holland
From: Irene Allen, Chief Accountant
Subject: Flexitime

You asked us to examine the financial implications of the flexitime system, and our general conclusions are as follows:

1 Overheads will increase because of the need for extra heating and lighting. Gas and electricity bills will rise by approximately 7%, but this may be offset by slightly lower insurance premiums because of the increased security of having staff on the premises longer. There may also be a reduction in photocopying costs if we do not need to use outside agencies so much.
2 Wages will not increase as long as staff who choose to work on Saturdays are not paid the overtime rate (standard wage plus 50%).
3 The clocking-in system will cost approximately £5,500 + VAT. This is a fixed cost and can be offset against tax.

A more detailed Costing Sheet Estimate is attached.

15
Personnel appointments

1 Words and definitions

Make words from the jumbled letters and match them with the definitions below.

a DLOUETCIISN   e EPRESNONL

b CNYCAVA   f RACERE MYASURM

c MRCUCIRUUL TVIEA   g NOVCRIEG TERELT

d EEREFRE

1 Another word for *appointment* or *post*.
2 Short profile of the job applicant at the beginning of a CV.
3 Person who writes a reference.
4 Document describing a job applicant's qualifications, work experience, and interests.
5 A job applicant may send this with a CV or application form.
6 Another word for *human resources*.
7 Application for a post that has not been advertised.

2 Follow-up to a job application

Robin Anakin sent an email to Glaston Potteries in response to an advertisement for an Administrator, but received no reply. Here he is following up with another email, but there are several mistakes in it relating to spelling, punctuation, paragraphing, language, and content. Rewrite the email in a more acceptable form.

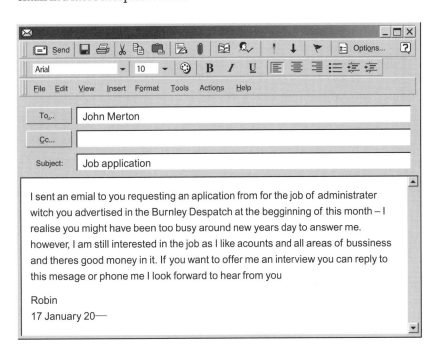

To... John Merton

Cc...

Subject: Job application

I sent an emial to you requesting an aplication from for the job of administrater witch you advertised in the Burnley Despatch at the begginning of this month – I realise you might have been too busy around new years day to answer me. however, I am still interested in the job as I like acounts and all areas of bussiness and theres good money in it. If you want to offer me an interview you can reply to this mesage or phone me I look forward to hear from you

Robin
17 January 20——

3 Job advertisement

Choose the best words from the options in brackets to complete the job advertisement below.

Personal Assistant to the Managing Director

We are looking for someone with **1**_____ (*current, fluent, spoken*) English and Italian, and preferably another language such as French or German. The **2**_____ (*secretary, interviewee, applicant*) should have at least five years' secretarial **3**_____ (*work, experience, employment*), preferably in an international environment. The work **4**_____ (*consists, contains, includes*) the usual secretarial **5**_____ (*work, duties, employment*), customer liaison, and **6**_____ (*doing, making, acting*) as an interpreter for the Managing Director, both here and elsewhere in Europe. For a(n) **7**_____ (*application form, CV, interview*), phone Paula Prentiss, the Personnel Manager, on (01223) 6814, Ext. 412, quoting **8**_____ (*number, reference, figure*) PP 391.

 International Publishing Ltd
60 Girton Street, Cambridge CB2 3EU

---

4 Covering letter

Carla Giuliani has decided to apply for the post of Personal Assistant to the Managing Director at International Publishing Ltd (see Exercise 3). She has completed the application form below. Using information from the job advertisement and the application form, write Carla's covering letter. Include the reference and the date, and remember to say:

- what job you are applying for
- why you would be suitable for the job, and why you are interested in it

---

 International Publishing Ltd
60 Girton Street, Cambridge CB2 3EU

APPLICATION FORM

Surname	*Giuliani*
Forename(s)	*Carla*
Address	*114 Ellesmere Walk, Finchley, London NW3 1DP*
Age	*28*
Date of birth	*4 January 19—*
Qualifications	*Degree in English and French (Università di Genova)*
	Secretarial Diploma (Pitman College, London)
Experience	*20— – 20— Secretary to Area Manager (N. Italy), Morgan Brice Ltd*
	20— – 20— PA to Sales Director, Morgan Brice Ltd
Languages	*Italian (mother tongue), English, French, German*
Office Skills	*Typing 60 w.p.m.*
	Shorthand 85 w.p.m.
	Familiar with Word, including spreadsheets
Hobbies and interests	*Tennis, swimming, horse riding, cinema*
Signature	*Carla Giuliani*
Date	*29 May 20—*

5 Invitation for an interview

Paula Prentiss has read Carla's application form and covering letter (see Exercise 4) and would like to interview her. As Paula Prentiss, write the letter inviting her to attend.

- Invite her to come for an interview at 14.30 on Thursday 18 June in Cambridge.
- Tell her that there will be a short Italian and French translation test before the interview.
- Send her a map with details, and tell her there are frequent trains to Cambridge from Liverpool Street.
- Ask her to phone you to confirm the date of the interview, or to arrange another one if she cannot attend on that day.

6 Making a job offer

Following a successful interview, Kevin Wheeler, Managing Director of International Publishing, would like the post of Personal Assistant to be offered to Carla (see Exercises 3–5) and has sent an email to Paula Prentiss. As Paula Prentiss, write the letter.

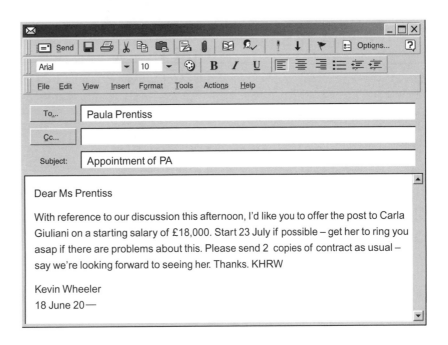

To... Paula Prentiss
Cc...
Subject: Appointment of PA

Dear Ms Prentiss

With reference to our discussion this afternoon, I'd like you to offer the post to Carla Giuliani on a starting salary of £18,000. Start 23 Juliy if possible – get her to ring you asap if there are problems about this. Please send 2 copies of contract as usual – say we're looking forward to seeing her. Thanks. KHRW

Kevin Wheeler
18 June 20—

Answer key

Note: For reasons of space, information such as addresses and dates is not set out at the top of most model letters, faxes, or emails in this Answer key (email signature blocks are also not included). If you are unfamiliar with the layout of a formal letter, a business fax, or a business email in English, you should work through the exercises in Units 1 and 2 of this Workbook before proceeding to the other units.

Unit 1
Letters, faxes, and emails

1 Letters: true or false?

1 F Yours sincerely
2 F carbon copy
3 F Dear Mr Smith
4 F chairman
5 T
6 F 2 June 2005
7 T
8 F Public Limited Company
9 T
10 T
11 T
12 F used for someone you know well

2 Order of addresses

1 Soundsonic Ltd
Warwick House
57–59 Warwick Street
London
SE23 1JF

2 Sig. D. Fregoni
Managing Director
Fregoni S.p.A.
Piazza Leonardo da Vinci 254
I-20133 Milano

3 Herr Heinz Bente
Chairman
Bente Spedition GmbH
Feldbergstr. 30
D-6000 Frankfurt 1

4 The Sales Manager
Sportique et Cie
201 rue Sambin
F–21000 Dijon

5 Mrs S. Moreno
Chief Accountant
Intercom
351 Avda Luis de Morales
E–41006 Sevilla

6 Ms Maria Nikolakaki
Nikitara 541
85100 Rhodes
Greece

7 Mrs Junko Shiratori
Excel Heights 501
7–3–8 Nakakasai
Edogawa-ku 139
Tokyo
Japan

8 The Transport Director
VHF Vehicles Ltd
301 Leighton Road
Kentish Town
London NW5 2QE

3 Letters: parts and layout

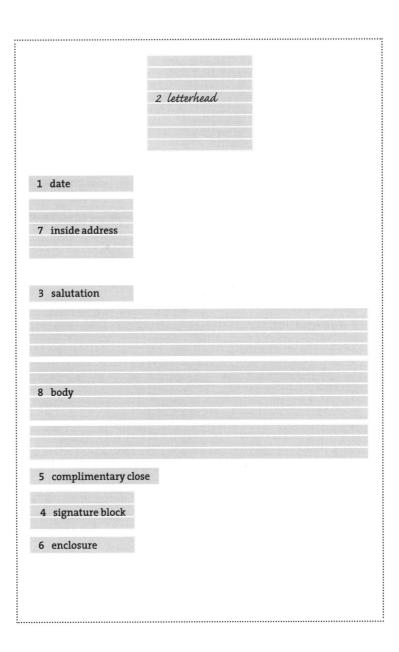

2 *letterhead*

1 date

7 inside address

3 salutation

8 body

5 complimentary close

4 signature block

6 enclosure

4 Faxes and emails: true or false?

1 T
2 F fax copy not valid
3 F facsimile
4 F not if you know recipient well
5 F use in informal email
6 T
7 F at
8 T use letter or card
9 F carbon copy
10 T
11 F use same principles as in letter
12 T

5 Fax transmission form

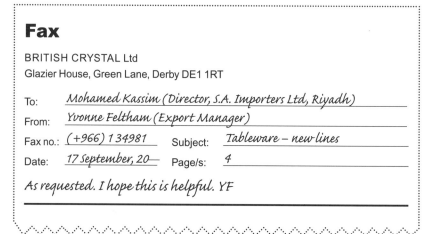

Fax

BRITISH CRYSTAL Ltd
Glazier House, Green Lane, Derby DE1 1RT

To: *Mohamed Kassim (Director, S.A. Importers Ltd, Riyadh)*

From: *Yvonne Feltham (Export Manager)*

Fax no.: *(+966) 1 34981*   Subject: *Tableware – new lines*

Date: *17 September, 20—*   Page/s: *4*

As requested. I hope this is helpful. YF

6 Email: request for further information

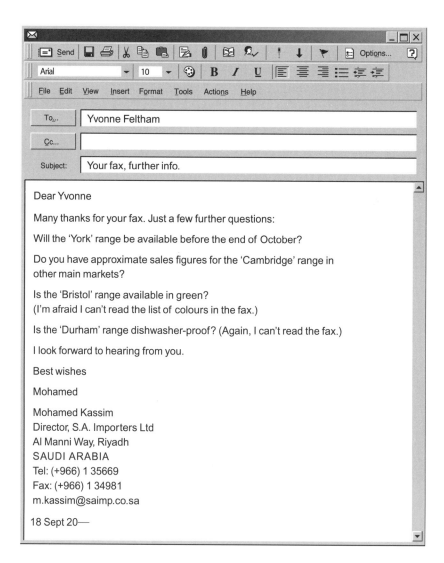

To... Yvonne Feltham

Cc...

Subject: Your fax, further info.

Dear Yvonne

Many thanks for your fax. Just a few further questions:

Will the 'York' range be available before the end of October?

Do you have approximate sales figures for the 'Cambridge' range in other main markets?

Is the 'Bristol' range available in green?
(I'm afraid I can't read the list of colours in the fax.)

Is the 'Durham' range dishwasher-proof? (Again, I can't read the fax.)

I look forward to hearing from you.

Best wishes

Mohamed

Mohamed Kassim
Director, S.A. Importers Ltd
Al Manni Way, Riyadh
SAUDI ARABIA
Tel: (+966) 1 35669
Fax: (+966) 1 34981
m.kassim@saimp.co.sa

18 Sept 20—

7 Email: checking

1 Change *Sir / Madam* to *Ms Bell*.
(He knows her name from the header information.)
2 First sentence should start with a capital letter, but the rest should be in lower case. (Remember, using capitals in emails is like shouting.)
3 *facilities*
4 Full stop after *facilities*.
5 *accommodate*
6 *July*
7 Delete *full board* (repeated later on)
8 *equipped*
9 *The*
10 *tariff*
11 *coffee*
12 *mid-morning*
13 *acceptable*
14 *sincerely*

8 Words and definitions

a 3 (blocked style)
b 6 (signature block)
c 2 (reference)
d 1 (enclosure)

e 5 (private and confidential)
f 8 (job title)
g 4 (yours sincerely)
h 7 (attachment)

Unit 2
Content and style

1 Typical sentences

1 We would be grateful for a reply as soon as possible.
2 Please find enclosed a cheque for £49.50.
3 If you need any further information, please contact us. /
Please contact us if you need any further information.
4 Thank you for your letter of 5 April. / Thank you for your letter of April 5.
5 We look forward to hearing from you.
6 I have pleasure in enclosing our spring catalogue and a price list.

2 Courtesy

Dear Sir

We are writing concerning the February balance of £567.00 on your account, which has been outstanding for three months. We wrote to you on 15 March and 4 April asking you to clear this balance, but did not receive a reply, which surprised us as you have been a regular customer for a number of years.

We would like to remind you that credit was offered on the understanding that balances would be cleared on the due dates; failure to do so could create difficulties for us with our own suppliers.

We are prepared to offer you a further ten days to clear the balance on this account, or explain why you cannot do so, otherwise we will, reluctantly, have to take legal action.

Yours faithfully

R. Lancaster (Mr)

3 Summarizing

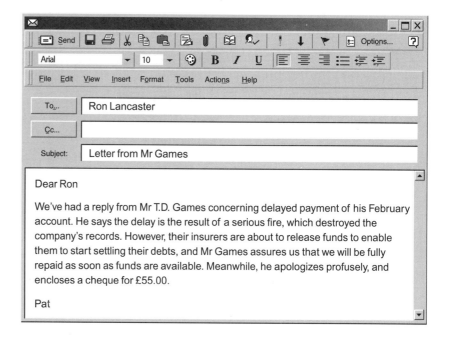

To... Ron Lancaster

Cc...

Subject: Letter from Mr Games

Dear Ron

We've had a reply from Mr T.D. Games concerning delayed payment of his February account. He says the delay is the result of a serious fire, which destroyed the company's records. However, their insurers are about to release funds to enable them to start settling their debts, and Mr Games assures us that we will be fully repaid as soon as funds are available. Meanwhile, he apologizes profusely, and encloses a cheque for £55.00.

Pat

4 Basing a letter on notes

Barnard Press Limited

183–7 Copwood Road
North Finchley
London N12 9PR
Telephone: +44 (0)20 8239 9653
Facsimile: +44 (0)20 8239 9754
Email: barnards@barnardpress.co.uk
www.barnardpress.co.uk

Our ref: SB/RW

1 March 20—

Sig. Claudio Bini
International Books
Via Santovetti 117/9
00045 Grottaferrata
Rome

Dear Sig. Bini,

Thank you for your enquiry of 15 February about readers for intermediate students of English.

Unfortunately, we have no readers in stock at the moment, but will be publishing a new series of intermediate-level readers, 'Storyworld', in the autumn. I have pleasure in enclosing a leaflet about the series, and our current catalogue.

We hope you will be interested in the new series, and look forward to hearing from you.

Yours sincerely
Rosalind Wood

p.p. Sarah Barnard

Sales Manager

5 Clear sequence

Dear Mr Jackson

NICOSIA COMPUTER TRAINING COURSE

Thank you for your letter of 18 May giving us the dates of your trip. I am writing with information about the arrangements we have made for your visit.

On Friday 9 June your flight to Larnaca will be met by our driver, who will take you to the Amathus Beach Hotel, where we have booked you in for the first two nights. We hope you enjoy your weekend at the hotel.

The driver will call for you at 17.00 on Sunday and drive you to the Training Centre at Nicosia. Most of the trainee operators will have had some experience of the new program by the time you arrive at the centre, but they will need a good deal of instruction on the more complex areas of the system.

The driver will pick you up from the Training Centre on Wednesday evening, at the end of the course, and take you back to the Amathus Beach Hotel, where I have booked you in for a further two nights. Unfortunately, Mr Charalambides will not be able to meet you in Larnaca on Thursday 15 June, as you requested, because he will be returning from a visit to our subsidiary in Spain. However, he will be back in the office the following day, so I have arranged for him to see you at 14.30.

Please could you confirm that you plan to return to London on the 18.30 flight on Friday 16, and also that the arrangements outlined here suit you?

I look forward to hearing from you.

Yours sincerely

Elena Theodorou

Training Manager

6 Planning

paragraph 1   Acknowledge letter
paragraph 2   Travel arrangements
              arrival time (Friday 9 June, Larnaca 15.30)
              departure time (Friday 16 June, 18.00, not 18.30)
paragraph 3   Training course No. of trainees? Photocopying facilities?
paragraph 4   Confirm time of meeting with Mr Charalambides OK
paragraph 5   Thank Ms Theodorou for her help

→

Dear Ms Theodorou

Thank you for your letter concerning the arrangements you have made for my trip to Cyprus in June. In general, I am very happy with them, but there are one or two things I would like to raise.

First, concerning the travel arrangements, please could you inform your driver that my flight on 9 June is scheduled to arrive in Larnaca at 15.30. And please note that my return flight to London on 16 June leaves Larnaca at 18.00, not 18.30.

With reference to the training course, how many trainees are there likely to be? Also, are there photocopying facilities at the Training Centre?

Finally, I can confirm that it will be convenient for me to meet Mr Charalambides at 14.30 on Friday 16 June.

Thank you for all your help.

Yours sincerely
Tom Jackson

Unit 3
Enquiries

1 Enquiry from a building company

Fax

**Clark Fitzpatrick Builders plc
Dunstable Road
Luton, Bedfordshire
LU2 3LM**

To:	Ms Doreen French
From:	Terry Spalding, Household Installations Ltd
Fax no:	01582 351711
Subject:	Kitchen units
Date:	3 April 20—
Page/s:	2

Dear Ms French

Thank you for your letter and the enclosed catalogue giving details of your kitchen units.

The main item we are interested in is the unit on page 22. It appears to meet all our specifications for the apartment block I described in my letter. I am sending herewith a plan of a typical apartment which gives the exact dimensions.

Before placing a firm order we would need samples of all materials used in the manufacture of the units. Could you please confirm that you guarantee all your products for two years against normal wear and tear? I would also be grateful for details of your terms regarding payment, and of any trade and quantity discounts.

If the price and quality of your products are satisfactory, we will place further orders as we have several projects at the planning stage.

Yours sincerely
Terry Spalding
Purchasing Manager

2 Words and definitions

a	5	(catalogue)	f	4	(showroom)
b	6	(estimate)	g	1	(subsidiary)
c	7	(tender)	h	8	(prospectus)
d	2	(customer)	i	10	(sale or return)
e	9	(wholesaler)	j	3	(quantity discount)

3 Polite requests

1 It is essential that the consignment is delivered before the end of September.
2 Could you please send us your catalogue and a price list?
3 As we intend to place a substantial order, we would like to know if you allow quantity discounts?
4 Please could you email us if you are unable to deliver the goods before Friday?
5 We would appreciate it if you could send us some samples.
6 We would be grateful if you could send one of your representatives here to give us an estimate.
7 We would be interested in seeing a demonstration of both models.
8 Would you be able to let us have twenty units on approval?
9 I am writing to enquire when you will be able to let us have the cheque?
10 As a rule, our suppliers allow us to settle by monthly statement.

4 Enquiry to a college

1	at	3	in	5	in	7	to	9	of	11	in
2	of	4	in	6	for	8	by	10	for	12	with

5 An application form

Student Application Form

International College • 145–8 Regents Road • Falmer • Brighton • BN1 9QN

APPLICANT

Family Name: _Ortega_

Other Names: _Maria_

Title Mr / Mrs / Miss / Ms: _Ms_   Age: _23_

Address: _Avda. San Antonio 501,_
80260 Bellaterra

Town / City: _Barcelona_   Country: _Spain_

Do you have a job or are you a student? _I am a student._

Job title / Subject of study: _Business Studies_

Name of business / university / college: _University of Barcelona_

Course applied for: _First Certificate_

Course dates: _3 January – 26 June 20—_

Are you paying your own fees, or is your company paying for you?
I am paying my own fees.

Will you find your own accommodation or do you want this to be arranged by the College? _I would like this to be arranged by the College._

Please tick how you found out about International College.

☐ Newspaper   ☑ Friend's recommendation

☐ Through your university / college   ☐ Other source: _____

Signature: _Maria Ortega_   Date: _10 November 20—_

6 Enquiry from a retailer

Cuisines Morreau S.A.
1150 boulevard Calbert
F—54015 Nancy Cedex
T l: +33 3 567349
Fax: +33 3 567350

R f: JFM/PS

28 June 20—

Sales Manager
Glaston Potteries Ltd
Clayfield
Burnley BB10 1RQ
UK

Dear Sir / Madam

I was impressed by your latest designs for oven-to-table ware advertised in the May edition of *International Homes*, and would be interested in retailing a selection from your range in my two shops here in Nancy.

It might be useful if I give you some idea of the terms on which I usually deal. I receive a 20% trade discount off ex-works prices from most of my suppliers, plus a 10% quantity discount if I place an order of over €10,000. I require delivery within two months of placing an order.

I would be grateful if you could send me a catalogue and price list, and also let me know what method of payment you would require.

I look forward to hearing from you soon.

Yours faithfully,

M. J.F. Morreau

Director

Unit 4
Replies and quotations

1 Reply to an enquiry

1, 2, 3, 4, 6, 7, 9, 11

2 Question forms

1 Please can you send me details of your prices?
2 Do you offer an after-sales service?
3 How long are the goods guaranteed for?
4 How soon can the goods be delivered?
5 What are your terms of payment?
6 Where can I buy the goods?
7 What sort of quantity discounts do you offer?
8 Can you please / Please can you send me your catalogue by express mail?

3 Words and definitions

a 2 (incoterm)
b 3 (net price)
c 1 (carriage forward)
d 7 (quotation)

e 5 (under separate cover)
f 6 (gross price)
g 4 (loyalty discount)

4 Reply to a request for information (1)

Dear Mr Russell

Thank you for your phone call of Thursday 4 March enquiring about hiring our delivery vans.

My colleague Ms Angela Smith, who took the call, said you were mainly interested in 5-ton vehicles like the 'Tobor', so I am enclosing our booklet 'Small Truck Hire', giving you details of our charges. These also appear on our website at www.vanhire.co.uk. You will notice that the summer months of June, July, and August are the least expensive and that we offer a 20% discount on weekend hire, starting Saturday at 08.00 and ending Sunday at 20.00.

Our main offices in the UK are in London and Birmingham, but we also have branches in France, Germany, and Italy. If you are thinking of hiring abroad you will find details on our website.

Please let me know if I can be of further help.

Yours sincerely

Michael Craddock

Transport Manager
Van Hire Unlimited

5 Incoterms

1 DDU (delivery duty unpaid) — c The seller pays all delivery costs, except for import duty, to a named destination.

2 CFR (cost and freight) — d The seller pays all delivery costs to a named destination, except for insurance.

3 CIF (cost, insurance, and freight) — f The seller pays all delivery costs to a named destination.

4 EXW (ex-works) — a The buyer pays all delivery costs once the goods have left the seller's factory or warehouse.

5 FAS (free alongside ship) — b The seller pays all delivery costs to the port.

6 FOB (free on board) — e The seller pays all delivery costs to when the goods are on board ship.

6 Reply to a request for information (2)

Dear Ms Croft

Thank you for your enquiry of 14 May about our fitness equipment.

I can confirm that only the highest-quality materials are used in all our equipment, and this is reflected in our 5-year guarantee.

Our prices are highly competitive, due to small profit margins, so I regret that we cannot offer credit terms. However, we do offer a 5% quantity discount on orders over €5,000.

I have pleasure in enclosing our catalogue and a price list. Please note that all prices are quoted CIF London.

If there is any further information you need, please contact us. Once again, thank you for your letter.

Yours sincerely

Birgit Lange

p.p. Gerd Busch

7 An estimate

Dear Mr Frost

Thank you for your telephone enquiry about upgrading the central heating system in your offices. I have pleasure in enclosing our estimate.

Draw down system	£40.00
Fit 7 thermostatic valves @ £20.00 per valve	£140.00
Fit 1 lockshield valve	£20.00
Fill and balance system	£50.00
Subtotal	£250.00
plus VAT @ 17.5%	£43.75

TOTAL £293.75

Prices quoted include materials and labour with VAT added as shown.

We confirm that we can complete the work before the end of September. If the work is to be carried out on a Saturday, you would need to add a total of £80.00 to this bill for overtime.

If you have any further questions, please contact me. I look forward to hearing from you.

Yours sincerely,

Steve Smart

MG Heating Engineers

Unit 5
Orders

1 Verbs used with *order*

1 We would like to *place* an order with you for 5,000 units.
2 As we are unable to supply the quantity you asked for, we shall have no objection if you prefer to *cancel* your order.
3 I am writing to *acknowledge* your order, which we received this morning, for 20 'Omega Engines'.
4 We are pleased to inform you that your order K451 has already been *despatched* from our depot.
5 Please *confirm* your order in writing, so we can inform our distribution depot.
6 Your order was *shipped* yesterday on the MV *Oxford*.
7 Unfortunately, we shall have to *refuse* your order unless payment is settled in cash.
8 I would like to reassure you that your order will be *made up* in our depot by staff who have experience in handling these delicate materials.

2 Placing an order: accompanying email

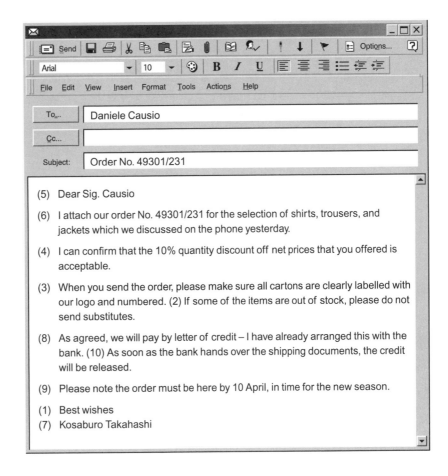

To... Daniele Causio

Cc...

Subject: Order No. 49301/231

(5) Dear Sig. Causio

(6) I attach our order No. 49301/231 for the selection of shirts, trousers, and jackets which we discussed on the phone yesterday.

(4) I can confirm that the 10% quantity discount off net prices that you offered is acceptable.

(3) When you send the order, please make sure all cartons are clearly labelled with our logo and numbered. (2) If some of the items are out of stock, please do not send substitutes.

(8) As agreed, we will pay by letter of credit – I have already arranged this with the bank. (10) As soon as the bank hands over the shipping documents, the credit will be released.

(9) Please note the order must be here by 10 April, in time for the new season.

(1) Best wishes
(7) Kosaburo Takahashi

3 Order form

Satex S.p.A.
ORDER FORM

Via di Pietra Papa, 00146 Roma

Date: _____

Name of company: Reiner GmbH

Order No: W6164

Telephone: +49 541 798252

Fax: +49 541 798253

Email: faustd@reiner.co.de

Address for delivery:

Wessumerstrasse 215–18,

D–4500 Osnabrück

Authorized: (D. Faust)

Item description	Cat. no.	Price € per item	Quantity	Total €
Shirts, plain white	S288	30	50	1,500
Shirts, plain blue	S289	30	50	1,500
Sweaters (V-neck), plain red	P112	40	20	800
Sweaters (V-neck), plain blue	P113	40	20	800

Amount due: € 4,600

Terms of payment: Banker s draft

Requested delivery date: Before 28 August 20—

4 Placing an order: covering letter

Sig. Daniele Causio
Sales Director
Satex S.p.A.
Via di Pietra Papa
00146 Roma

Dear Sig. Causio

Order No. W6164

Thank you for your letter of 1 July, and the catalogue and price list.

Please find enclosed the above order. We would like to remind you that we expect delivery before 28 August, i.e. within six weeks. We will pay by banker's draft as soon as we receive the shipping documents.

If any of the items we have ordered are not available, please do not send substitutes. And please could you email Herr Faust if there are any problems with delivery?

We look forward to receiving acknowledgement of this order.

Yours sincerely

Beatrice Mey

pp. Dieter Faust

Buying Manager

5 Acknowledging an order

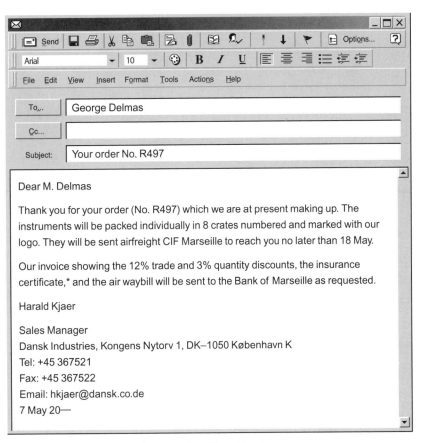

To... George Delmas

Cc...

Subject: Your order No. R497

Dear M. Delmas

Thank you for your order (No. R497) which we are at present making up. The instruments will be packed individually in 8 crates numbered and marked with our logo. They will be sent airfreight CIF Marseille to reach you no later than 18 May.

Our invoice showing the 12% trade and 3% quantity discounts, the insurance certificate,* and the air waybill will be sent to the Bank of Marseille as requested.

Harald Kjaer

Sales Manager
Dansk Industries, Kongens Nytorv 1, DK–1050 København K
Tel: +45 367521
Fax: +45 367522
Email: hkjaer@dansk.co.de
7 May 20—

*The comma between *certificate* and *and* is optional.

6 Delay in delivery

1	concerning	6	reach
2	placed	7	care
3	apologize	8	consignment
4	shortage	9	according
5	taken on	10	prevent

7 Refusing an order

1 d ✓   2 e ✓   3 ✓ b   4 a ✓   5 ✓ c

8 Words and definitions

a	6 (compliments slip)	e	8 (air waybill)
b	3 (invoice)	f	7 (ship)
c	1 (forwarding agent)	g	2 (covering letter)
d	5 (settlement)	h	4 (advice note)

Unit 6
Payment

1 Invoice

Clayfield | Burnley | BB10 1RQ

GLASTON
POTTERIES LTD

Telephone + 44 (0)1282 46125
Facsimile + 44 (0)1282 63182
Email accounts@glaston.co.uk
www.glaston.com

J. F. Morreau
1150 boulevard Calbert
F–54015 Nancy Cedex

9 May 20—

Your order No. 3716

Quantity	Description	Cat. No.	£ each	£
10	Lotus	L305	35	350
20	Wedgwood	W218	43	860

CIF _15%_   181.50

Less _____ discount off net price   1,028.50

Total _____

Payment due within 28 days of date of invoice.

E&OE

Registered No. 716481
VAT Reg. No. 133 53431 08

2 Statement of account

HOMEMAKERS

54–59 Riverside, Cardiff CF1 1JW
Telephone: +44 (0)29 20 49721
Fax: +44 (0)29 20 49937

statement

To: R. Hughes & Son Ltd, 21 Mead Road, Swansea, West Glamorgan, 3ST 1DR

Date	Item	Debit	Credit	Balance
1 May	Account Rendered			461.00
5 May	Inv. 771/2	781.00		1,242.00
7 May	Cheque		300.00	942.00
12 May	C/N 216		285.00	657.00
16 May	Inv. 824/2	302.00		959.00
18 May	Cheque		200.00	759.00
23 May	D/N 306	100.00		859.00

Terms:
Cash discount 3% if paid within 10 days

3 Request for more time to settle an account

Dear Mr Merton

I am sorry that at present I am unable to settle your invoice dated 9 May for my order No. 3716. The reason for this is that my stockroom was flooded after recent heavy rain, and much of the stock damaged or destroyed.

Unfortunately, I am unable to pay any of my suppliers until I receive compensation from my insurers. They have promised me this within the next four weeks. As soon as I receive payment, I will settle the invoice in full.

I hope that you will understand the situation.

Yours sincerely

Jean Morreau (M.)

4 Crossword

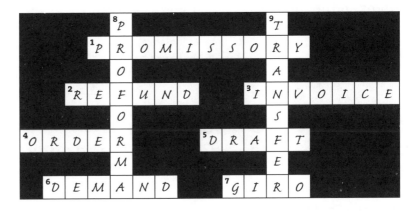

5 Request for payment

1 account
2 for
3 clear
4 on
5 offer
6 with
7 balance
8 within

6 Reply to request for payment

```
3 May 20—
Ms Helen Stuart
Chief Accountant
UK Cycles Ltd
Borough House
Borough Road
Cleveland
TS1 3BA
UK

Dear Ms Stuart
```

Account No. VS 301632

```
Thank you for your letters of 25 March and 28 April regarding the
delay in settling our account with you.

Unfortunately, a recent fire at our Head Office has destroyed a
great deal of our computer data, with the result that all
correspondence with both suppliers and customers has been
disrupted. I am afraid that we will need time to return to our
normal routine.

Would it be possible for you to allow us a further 30 days to settle?
By that time, our insurance company will have released compensation,
and we can pay the outstanding amount in full.

I would be most grateful if you could allow us this extra time.

Yours sincerely,

Karl Janssen

Managing Director
```

7 Formal and informal English

1 (F) and a (I)   3 (F) and b (I)   5 (F) and c (I)
2 (I) and d (F)   4 (F) and e (I)

8 Words and definitions

a 3 (current account)   f 2 (due date)
b 9 (sight draft)   g 1 (protest)
c 6 (balance)   h 5 (remittance)
d 4 (bank transfer)   i 7 (statement of account)
e 10 (documentary credit)   j 8 (debit note)

Unit 7
Complaints and adjustments

1 Formal and informal English

1 b ✓   2 ✓ h   3 ✓ g   4 ✓ a   5 c ✓   6 d ✓   7 e ✓   8 ✓ f

2 Complaint about damage

1 complain   4 handled   7 wear   10 insurers
2 invoice   5 rusty   8 consignment 11 carriage forward
3 crates   6 torn   9 inspecting   12 refund

3 Complaint about late delivery

 ISTITUTO DI MEDICINA

Viale Bracci
1–61001 Siena
Telefono: +39 0586 43-74-25
Fax: +39 0586 43-74-26
Email: clotti@imed.ac.it

15 June 20—

Mr H. Toda
Sales Manager
Nihon Instruments
12–18 Wakakusa-cho
Hagashi-Osaka-Shi
Osaka-fu
Japan

Dear Mr Toda

AWB 4156/82

We are writing to point out that the above delivery, which arrived yesterday, was a week late. This is the second time we have had to write to you on this subject, and we cannot allow the situation to continue. We have already explained that it is essential for medical equipment to arrive on due dates as late delivery could create a very serious problem.

Unless we have your firm guarantee on the promptness of all future deliveries, we will have to look for another supplier. Please could you confirm this before we place our next order?

Yours sincerely

Carlo Lotti (Sig.)

Head of Administration

4 Reply to complaint about damage

Dear Sr Méndez

Thank you for your letter of 15 October concerning the damage to a consignment of garden furniture against invoice No. G3190/1. I can confirm that the goods were checked before they left our warehouse, so it appears that the damage occurred during shipment.

Please could you return the goods to us, carriage forward? We will send a refund by banker s draft as soon as we receive them.

In your letter you mention two further crates. Could you let me know whether you have received these safely?

Please accept my apologies for the inconvenience caused.

Yours sincerely

Brian Harrison

5 Reply to complaint about late delivery

(9) Dear Mr Lotti

(1) **Consignment no. AWB 4156/82**

(6) Thank you for your letter of 15 June concerning late delivery of the above consignment.

(8) We understand how important prompt deliveries are to our customers. (3) However, the two orders you mentioned were sent to our factory rather than our administrative offices at the above address.

(4) We would like to take this opportunity of reminding you that to avoid delay in future all orders should be sent to our office address.

(2) I trust that this will clarify the situation, and look forward to continued good trading with you.

(10) Yours sincerely

(7) Hirio Toda (Mr)

(5) Sales Manager

6 Complaint about accounting errors

Mrs B. Grevon
Accounts Department
Excel Stationers Ltd
28 Langley Estate
Templetown
London WC3 7AL

22 November 20—

Dear Mrs Grevon

Invoice no. 3910

We have received the above invoice, but notice it contains a number of errors.

1. 12 writing pads @ 2.80 each total £33.60, not £35.30
2. 3 boxes pens @ 1.50 each total £4.50, not £3.50
3. 8 reams multi-purpose paper @ 3.90 each total £31.20, not £33.20

The correct final total is therefore £86.90, not £89.60.

We will settle the account as soon as we receive a corrected invoice.

As we have been sent incorrect invoices several times in the past, I regret to tell you that it will be necessary for us to change our suppliers if this happens again.

Yours sincerely

Unit 8
Credit

1 Formal and informal English

1 Thank you for forwarding the documents so *promptly*.
2 We feel that *sufficient* time has *elapsed* for you to *settle*.
3 I am writing to *request* open account facilities.
4 We would like to remind you that this information is highly *confidential*.
5 Your quarterly settlement is three weeks *overdue*.
6 We are pleased to *inform* you that the credit facilities you asked for are *acceptable*.
7 Our prices are very *competitive*.

2 Agreeing to credit

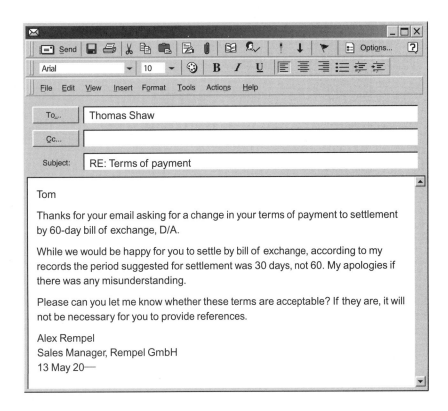

To... Thomas Shaw

Cc...

Subject: RE: Terms of payment

Tom

Thanks for your email asking for a change in your terms of payment to settlement by 60-day bill of exchange, D/A.

While we would be happy for you to settle by bill of exchange, according to my records the period suggested for settlement was 30 days, not 60. My apologies if there was any misunderstanding.

Please can you let me know whether these terms are acceptable? If they are, it will not be necessary for you to provide references.

Alex Rempel
Sales Manager, Rempel GmbH
13 May 20—

3 Request for a reference

1 to	3 of	5 of	7 on/by	9 for
2 on	4 at	6 for	8 to	10 at

4 Reply to request for a reference

Dear Sra. Gómez

I am replying to your enquiry of 18 May concerning D.L. Cromer Ltd.

The company has an excellent reputation in the UK and has been a customer of ours for a number of years. Their credit limit with us is slightly lower than the level you mentioned, but we have always found that they settle on, or before, due dates.

We would be grateful if you could treat this information in the strictest confidence.

Yours sincerely

Gerald MacFee

Credit Controller

5 Unfavourable reply

Dear Ms Allard

I am replying to your enquiry of 19 September about *one of our mutual business associates.*

We have allowed *that company* credit in the past, but *nowhere near the amount* you mentioned. We have also found that they need *several* reminders before clearing their account.

Please treat this information in the strictest confidence.

Yours sincerely

P.M. Lord

Accountant

6 Words and definitions

a 2 (bad debt)	c 3 (bill of exchange)	e 6 (reference)
b 4 (credit rating)	d 5 (default)	f 1 (credit facilities)

Unit 9
Banking

1 Reporting verbs

1 thank	3 refuse	5 promise	7 explain
2 suggest	4 advise	6 admit	8 apologize

2 Word forms

1 endanger	4 insurance	7 confirmation	9 expansion
2 completing	5 overdraft	8 signature	10 reference
3 payable	6 arrangement		

3 Bill of exchange

At **1** *60 days after date* pay this **2** *sola* Bill of Exchange
2 _____ to the order of Number 40031 3021

Exchange for **3** *$28,000* **4** *28 February 20—*
5 *Hartley-Mason Inc.*
6 *US dollars twenty-eight thousand*

Value Received **7** *payable at the current rate of exchange for bankers' drafts in London* placed to account

To
8 *Glough and Book Motorcyles Ltd*
31–37 Trades Street
Nottingham
NG13AA

For and on behalf of
9 *Hartley-Mason Inc.*
618 West and Vine Street
Chicago
Illinois

Signed
9 *J.R. Mason*
President

4 Request for a loan

To: The Board of Directors
From: John Steele
Subject: Bridging loan, RG Logistics Ltd
Date: 19 September 20—

STRICTLY CONFIDENTIAL

I had a meeting with Mr Richard Grey, of RG Logistics Ltd, on 17 September. He admitted that his company has had difficulties recently, but he would like to expand his fleet by buying a further two second-hand trucks, and requested an extension on his loan to cover the investment.

I informed him that we would have to refuse an extension on his existing loan, but explained that we may be able to offer a bridging loan. He suggested that he would need around £50,000, but he is confident that the revenue generated by the extra trucks would enable him to repay the loan within a year. He is able only to offer the trucks themselves as security.

I promised him that I would consult you this week.

5 Refusing a loan

Dear Mr Grey

Further to our meeting on 17th September, I regret that we will not be able to offer you a bridging loan. The Board of Directors have asked me to inform you that it is the bank's policy only to offer substantial loans against negotiable securities such as shares or bonds.

You may be able to raise the capital you need from another source, for example a finance corporation. However, I should warn you that their interest rates are likely to be significantly higher than ours.

Once again, I regret that we have to disappoint you in this matter, but hope that we may be of more help in the future.

Yours sincerely

John Steele

Manager

6 Words and definitions

a	1	(endorse)	e	6	(days after sight)
b	5	(documentary credit)	f	2	(merchant bank)
c	3	(certificate of origin)	g	7	(overhead)
d	4	(clean bill)	h	8	(sight draft)

7 Abbreviations

1 bill of exchange
2 documents against payment
3 letter of credit
4 documents against acceptance
5 errors and omissions excepted
6 documentary credit
7 carriage paid
8 days after sight
9 international money order
10 carriage forward

8 Documentary credit 1

Letter from the confirming bank to the exporters

1	acting	3	opened	5	charges	7	draw
2	inform	4	valid	6	documents	8	settle

9 Documentary credit 2

Letter from the exporters to the confirming bank

Dear M. Diderot

L/C No. 340895/AGL

Thank you for your advice of 8 July. We have now effected shipment to BestValue and enclose the shipping documents you requested and our draft for €5,300.

Please will you accept the draft and remit the proceeds to our account at the Banque de Commerce, 28 rue Gaspart-André, 69002, Lyon.

Yours sincerely

James Freeland

Château Wines

Enc. Air waybill
     Invoice CIF London
     Insurance certificate

Unit 10
Agents and agencies

1 Find the keyword

1 STOCK EXCHANGE	7 NET
2 CONFIRMING	8 COMMODITY
3 SOLE AGENT	9 DEL CREDERE
4 COMMISSION	10 BUYING HOUSE
5 PRINCIPAL	11 MARKET
6 FACTORING	12 keyword = CONSIGNMENT

2 Phrasal verbs

1 work out	3 draw up	5 turn down	7 fill in
2 take on	4 back up	6 make out	8 take up

3 Offer of an agency

1 said	4 settle	7 offer	9 researchers
2 approval	5 trial	8 cost	10 current
3 sole	6 extend		

4 Reply to an offer of an agency

1 c   2 a   3 c   4 c   5 a   6 b

```
Sig. Pietro Grazioli
Chairman
Grazioli S.p.A.
Via Gradenigo 134
50133 Firenze
Italy

31 October 20—

Dear Sig. Grazioli

Thank you for your letter of 23 October.

I can confirm that we would be interested in representing you, but
not on a sole agency basis, as this would restrict our sales. Also,
our usual terms are a 10% commission on ex-works prices and 75% of
the advertising costs.

However, we were very impressed by the high quality of the products
in your catalogue. If you are able to revise your terms, we would be
interested in receiving a draft contract.

I look forward to hearing from you.

Yours sincerely

Otto Grassmann

Grassmann AG
```

5 Request for an agency

1 recommendation	4 principals	7 rates	10 del credere
2 manufacturers	5 freight	8 documentation	11 offer
3 terms	6 factory	9 commission	12 brochure

6 Reply to a request for an agency

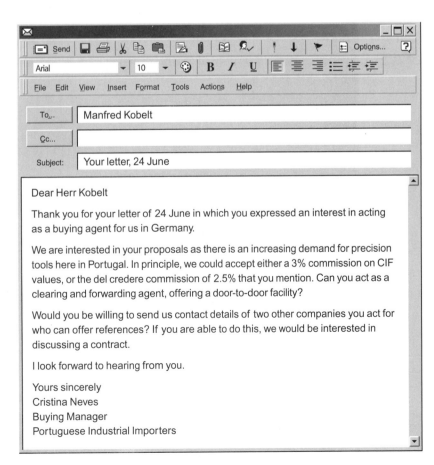

Dear Herr Kobelt

Thank you for your letter of 24 June in which you expressed an interest in acting as a buying agent for us in Germany.

We are interested in your proposals as there is an increasing demand for precision tools here in Portugal. In principle, we could accept either a 3% commission on CIF values, or the del credere commission of 2.5% that you mention. Can you act as a clearing and forwarding agent, offering a door-to-door facility?

Would you be willing to send us contact details of two other companies you act for who can offer references? If you are able to do this, we would be interested in discussing a contract.

I look forward to hearing from you.

Yours sincerely
Cristina Neves
Buying Manager
Portuguese Industrial Importers

Unit 11
Transportation and shipping

1 Two-word terms

1	forwarding agent	5	air waybill
2	bulk carrier	6	all risks
3	charter party	7	shipping note
4	delivery note	8	shipping mark

2 Formal and informal English

1 Please fill in the despatch form and send it to us with the consignment.
2 If you have any queries, please do not hesitate to contact me.
3 I have checked with our Despatch Department and their records show that the crockery left here in perfect condition.
4 Please quote for collection of a consignment of ten armchairs from the above address and delivery to R. Hughes & Son Ltd, Swansea.
5 We estimate the loss on invoice value to be £300.00 and we are claiming compensation for that amount.
6 Would you prefer us to return the goods to you, or to hold them for inspection?

3 Enquiry to a forwarding agent

1	to	3	for	5	in	7	of	9	to	11	of
2	by	4	for	6	of	8	of	10	by	12	in

4 Forwarding agent's reply

Dear Mr Lang

Thank you for your fax of 10 November enquiring about our freight charges.

I enclose our tariff list for shipments which includes all transport, customs, and documentation charges. I think you will find that these rates are highly competitive. In addition, I can confirm that we have extensive experience in handling fragile consignments.

If you have any further questions, please contact me and I will be very pleased to help.

I look forward to hearing from you.

Yours sincerely

Bill Crowley

5 Words and definitions

a 5 (payload)
b 8 (endorse)
c 7 (claused)
d 3 (multimodal)
e 2 (receipt)
f 1 (consolidation)
g 4 (shipbroker)
h 6 (container)

6 Enquiry to a container company

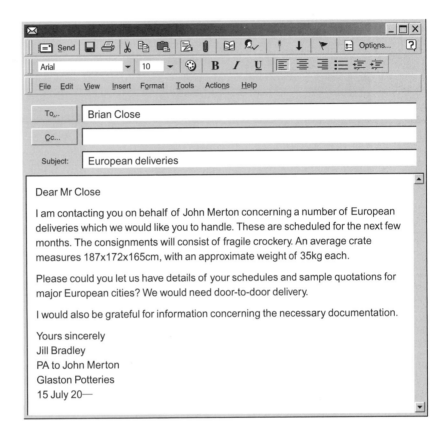

To... Brian Close

Cc...

Subject: European deliveries

Dear Mr Close

I am contacting you on behalf of John Merton concerning a number of European deliveries which we would like you to handle. These are scheduled for the next few months. The consignments will consist of fragile crockery. An average crate measures 187x172x165cm, with an approximate weight of 35kg each.

Please could you let us have details of your schedules and sample quotations for major European cities? We would need door-to-door delivery.

I would also be grateful for information concerning the necessary documentation.

Yours sincerely
Jill Bradley
PA to John Merton
Glaston Potteries
15 July 20—

7 Container company's reply

1 full stop after *yesterday*
2 *schedules*, not *shedules*
3 *tomorrow*, not *tommorow*
4 *suggest*, not *sugest*
5 *export cargo packing instructions* in lower-case, not capitals
6 *Consignments*, not *Consignment*
7 *sample*, not *smaple*
8 *responsibilities*, not *responsibilites*
9 *all risk* or *all-risk*, not *allrisk*
10 *are any other details*, not *is any other details*

Unit 12
Insurance

1 Terms used in insurance

1 insurance
2 syndicates
3 policy
4 indemnified
5 premium
6 Lloyd's
7 proposal
8 claim
9 fidelity
10 adjuster

2 Request for comprehensive insurance

1 large
2 which
3 to
4 would like
5 supply
6 covering
7 include
8 kind
9 premises
10 competitive
11 consider
12 soon

3 Reply to request for
   comprehensive insurance

18 February 20—

Peter Hind
Company Secretary
Humboldt Exporters Ltd
Exode House
115 Tremona Road
Southampton SO9 4XY

Dear Mr Hind

Thank you for your letter of 15 February enquiring about
comprehensive cover for your warehouse at Dock Road, Southampton.

I enclose details of two fully comprehensive industrial policies
which offer the sort of cover you describe in your letter. It would
probably be best if one of our agents called on you to discuss which
of these policies would best suit your requirements.

If you would like to arrange an appointment, please call my
secretary, Natalie Weston, on 01273 547231, extension 12.

We hope to hear from you in the near future.

Yours sincerely

Gerald Croft

Regional Manager

Encl. Leaflets IP3, IP4

4 Claim for fire damage

From: Peter Hind
To: Gerald Croft
Subject: Warehouse fire
Date: 7 October 20—

Policy No. 439178/D
I regret to inform you that fire broke out in our Southampton warehouse early yesterday
morning. This resulted in extensive damage, to the value of approximately £7,000, to
textiles stored for shipment.

The Fire Service has provided evidence that the fire was caused by an electrical fault.

Please could you send me the necessary claim forms as soon as possible?

Peter Hind

5 Request for open cover

1 May 20—

Sugden & Able
Insurance Brokers
63 Grover Street
Manchester M5 6LD

Dear Sir / Madam

We are a large engineering company exporting machine parts
worldwide, and have a contract to supply a Middle Eastern customer
for the next two years.

As the parts we will be supplying are similar in nature and are
going to the same destination over this period, we would prefer to
insure them under an open cover policy.

Would you be willing to provide open cover for £500,000 against
all risks for this period?

I look forward to hearing from you.

Yours faithfully

Jack Turner

Shipping Manager

**6 Reply to request
for open cover**

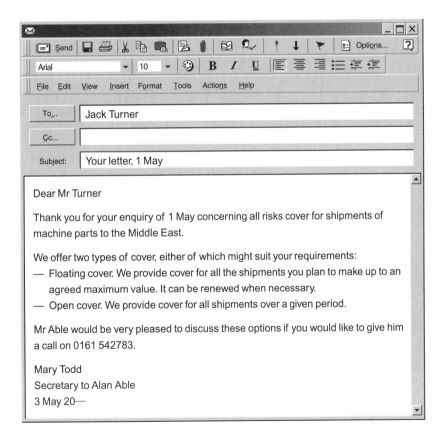

To... Jack Turner

Cc...

Subject: Your letter, 1 May

Dear Mr Turner

Thank you for your enquiry of 1 May concerning all risks cover for shipments of
machine parts to the Middle East.

We offer two types of cover, either of which might suit your requirements:
— Floating cover. We provide cover for all the shipments you plan to make up to an
  agreed maximum value. It can be renewed when necessary.
— Open cover. We provide cover for all shipments over a given period.

Mr Able would be very pleased to discuss these options if you would like to give him
a call on 0161 542783.

Mary Todd
Secretary to Alan Able
3 May 20—

Unit 13
Miscellaneous correspondence

1 Prepositions

Please send the tickets for my attention / by return.
May I offer you my best wishes for Eid Al-Fittr.
She offers her apologies for the inconvenience.
I would like to speak on effective website design.
I hope to return the favour on some future occasion.
Please confirm these reservations by return / for my attention.
We will need a room with full conference facilities.

2 Formal and informal English

1 He sends his apologies, and hopes to be able to attend on another occasion.
2 I was sorry to hear that your brother is ill.
3 I would like to congratulate you on being elected Chairman of the company.
4 Mr Norman would like to make an appointment to see you next week about the contract.
5 Unfortunately, Mr Chung will not be able to keep his appointment with you on Friday.
6 We would like to invite you to our Sales Conference on 18 March.
7 I would like to thank you for assisting me while I was in Hamburg last week.
8 I look forward to seeing you on Friday.

3 Conference facilities

Dear Sir / Madam

We are planning a Sales Conference on 8 and 9 December this year and are looking for a hotel which can offer us accommodation and conference facilities for forty delegates.

We require executive-grade accommodation for twenty-seven delegates on the nights of 7 and 8 December, and a conference room with full seating, presentation platform, public address system, PowerPoint, and facilities for recording from 09.00 to 18.00 on both days of the conference. We would also like morning coffee and biscuits at 11.00, bar facilities, a buffet lunch, and tea with snacks at 16.00.

If you can meet these requirements, I would be grateful if you could send me full details of your rates and facilities.

Yours faithfully

Lynn Paul

PA to Diane Taylor

4 Hotel reservation

Fax

Data Unlimited plc
Data House
Chertsey Road
Twickenham
TW1 1EP
Tel: +44 (0)20 81 460259
Fax: +44 (0)20 81 985132

To: The Manager, Royal Hotel
From: Lynn Paul
Fax: 01372 908754
Subject: Additional reservations
Date: 3 December
Page/s: 1

Dear Sir / Madam

I would like, if possible, to make reservations for the nights of 7 and 8 December for two more delegates attending our Sales Conference. Their names are Charles Bickford and Claire Ramal. Preferably, the reservations should be for executive-grade rooms.

I would be grateful if you could let me know by return if you can accommodate them.

My apologies for the short notice.

Lynn Paul

PA to Diane Taylor

5 Invitation

1 would like
2 wonder
3 speakers
4 appreciate

5 affecting
6 let
7 speak
8 Enclosed

6 Accepting an invitation

Dear Mr House

Thank you for your letter inviting me to speak at your annual dinner on 15 February.

I would like to accept your kind invitation. In my talk, I would like to focus on the effects that the euro is having on the cost of raw materials. I will send you a transcript next week and would welcome any comments or suggestions you would like to make.

I look forward very much to meeting you on 15 February.

Yours sincerely

Gunther Boldt

Chairman

Unit 14
Memos and reports

1 Formal and informal English

1 c ✓ 2 g ✓ 3 ✓ e 4 h ✓ 5 a ✓ 6 ✓ b 7 ✓ d 8 ✓ f

2 Memo about documentry credits

Memo

To: All Documentary Credit Department Staff
From: Finance Director
Date: 20 March 20—
Subject: Verification of Documentary Credits

Would all staff be extremely careful in checking documentary credits in future. Over the past year £250,000 has been lost in paying clients compensation for mistakes in documentary credits.

Pay particular attention to the following points:

- Check all transport documents, insurance certificates, invoices and customs clearance certificates.
- Check bills of exchange and letters of credit.
- Check the spelling in the names of the parties is correct.
- Check that places of departure and destinations are correct.
- Check the right amounts for the transactions are listed and the correct currencies have been written in.

3 Memo about fraud

Memo

National Stores plc
528 Marylebone Road
London W1B 3MC

To: Sales staff
From: Fred Hanbury, Chief Accountant
Date: 18th November 20—
Subject: Payments by cheque

The value of bad cheques presented in this store over the past year amounts to over £50,000. This problem cannot be eliminated, but you can help reduce it significantly by taking the following measures:
1 Examine cheques to see that they have been completed properly.
2 Carefully match signatures on cheque cards with those on cheques.
3 Write the cheque card number and expiry date on the back of the cheque.
4 If you are unsure about a cheque, contact a supervisor immediately.

Terry Fairman

Chief Accountant

4 Reports: past tenses

EXTRACT 1

1 has been exporting
2 opened
3 remained
4 moved
5 have been negotiating

EXTRACT 2

6 has been losing
7 rose
8 has been operating
9 occurred
10 have been having

EXTRACT 3

11 was
12 felt
13 remained
14 have been falling
15 have been returning
16 have been increasing

5 Report on introduction of flexitime

To: The Board of Directors
From: John Holland, Company Secretary
Date   16 March 20—
Subject: Proposed flexitime system

Management proposes to introduce a flexitime system for all staff. Under this system, staff would be able to choose their hours of work between 07.00 and 21.00, and have a weekday off in lieu of Saturday if they prefer.

Advantages to the company

There are several advantages to the company. For example, increased working hours would mean that overseas clients in different time zones would find it easier to contact us, and clients could contact us on Saturdays. Pressure on office equipment such as photocopiers would be relieved and therefore efficiency would be improved.

Advantages to staff

The two most significant advantages to staff are that they would be able to avoid rush hour travel, and they would also be able to spend more time with their families. This is likely to lead to a significant improvement in morale and productivity.

Financial costs and benefits

The financial cost of such a scheme is considerable. The initial cost of installing a clocking-in system would be approximately £5,500 + VAT. (However, this is a fixed cost and can be offset against tax.) The estimated increase in overheads would be 7%, but this can be offset against benefits such as lower insurance premiums and photocopying costs. There is also, as noted above, likely to be a substantial increase in productivity.

Conclusion

The idea is very popular among the staff: an overwhelming majority of 87% are in favour of it, although it should be noted that a significant number (48%) are not in favour of a clocking-in system, so this would need to be introduced carefully.

After careful analysis of the information provided, I conclude that the introduction of a flexitime system would be viable financially. I therefore recommend its introduction within the next six months.

Unit 15
Personnel appointments

1 Words and definitions

a 7 (unsolicited)
b 1 (vacancy)
c 4 (curriculum vitae)
d 3 (referee)

e 6 (personnel)
f 2 (career summary)
g 5 (covering letter)

2 Follow-up to
a job application

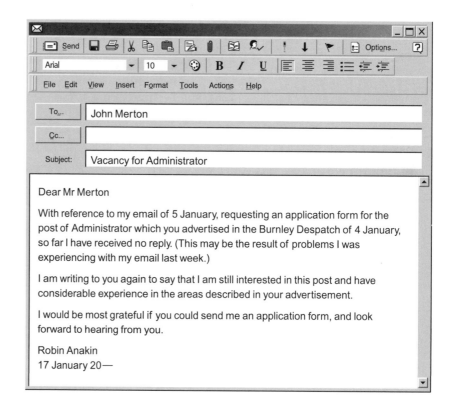

3 Job advertisement

1 fluent
2 applicant
3 experience
4 includes

5 duties
6 acting
7 application form
8 reference

4 Covering letter

Your ref. PP391

29 May 20—

Dear Ms Prentiss

I would like to apply for the vacancy of PA to the Managing Director.

As you will see from my application form, Italian is my mother tongue and I studied English and French at university. I also speak good German. In my current job as PA to the Sales Director of Morgan Brice Ltd, I accompany her on trips to our offices in Italy and France, where I am often required to translate and interpret.

I am very interested in this post as I would like to develop my career in an international environment. On a more personal level, I would also like, if possible, to move away from London.

I look forward to hearing from you.

Yours sincerely

Carla Giuliani (Ms)

Enc. Application form

5 Invitation for an interview

Dear Ms Giuliani

Thank you for your application of 29 May for the post of PA to the Managing Director.

We would like you to come for interview in Cambridge on Thursday 18 June at 14.30. There will be a short Italian and French translation test before the interview. I enclose a map with details of how to reach us by car. Alternatively, there are frequent trains to Cambridge from Liverpool Street.

I would be grateful if you could phone me on 01223 6814, Ext. 412 to confirm that you will be able to attend, or to arrange an alternative date if you cannot attend on that day.

I look forward to hearing from you.

Yours sincerely

Paula Prentiss (Ms)

Personnel Manager

6 Making a job offer

Dear Ms Giuliani

I have much pleasure in offering you the post of Personal Assistant to Kevin Wheeler.

I can confirm that your starting salary will be £18,000. We would like, if possible, for your employment to commence on 23 July. Can you please ring me as soon as possible if you are unable to start on this date?

Please sign both copies of the enclosed Contract of Employment and return one to me, keeping the other for your records.

We look forward to welcoming you to the company.

Yours sincerely

Paula Prentiss

Personnel Manager

Enc. Contract of Employment (x2)